MONAHSETAH, RESISTANCE

AND OTHER MARKINGS ON TURTLE'S BACK

FIRST EDITION, 2017

Monahsetah, Resistance
and Other Markings on Turtle's Back

Cover Art
"Cheyenne Women Returning to Camp with Firewood."
The Miriam and Ira D. Wallach Division of Art, Prints and Photographs:
Photography Collection, The New York Public Library. The New York
Public Library Digital Collections. 1860 - 1920.
http://digitalcollections.nypl.org/items/510d47d9-aa45-a3d9-e040-e00a18064a99

Author Photo
Maurice Kenny by White Pine Press.
Chad Sweeney by Jennifer K. Sweeney

This publisher is a proud member of

[clmp]

COUNCIL OF LITERARY MAGAZINES & PRESSES
w w w . c l m p . o r g

MONAHSETAH, RESISTANCE
AND OTHER MARKINGS ON TURTLE'S BACK

Lyric History, Poems and Essays

by

Maurice Kenny

Edited by Chad Sweeney

MONGREL EMPIRE PRESS
NORMAN, OKLAHOMA, UNITED STATES OF AMERICA

2017

CONTENTS

INTRODUCTION

It took courage to truly observe the land of my birth where part of my blood was hated, and the other part was imported into a land knee deep in genocide and bloody with racism, sexism and homophobia, blockades to liberty and happiness let alone sexual fulfillment.

. . . .

> *Who do I want revenge against*
> *and for what?*
> *Who is my enemy?*
> *I have eaten my own heart many times*
> *—Maurice Kenny*

Maurice Kenny had long criticized historical reductions of Native Americans as either militant aggressors or victims, as savage primitives or noble clichés, a history obsessed by military theater in one descending trajectory of conflict and erasure. Such history, written by European Americans, remained willfully ignorant of the Native "circle of life" vis-à-vis art, dance, song, oral literature, food, love, family, ritual, language and loyalty, as daily acts of cultural celebration, survival, resilience, and resistance. Kenny dedicated much of his life to restoring and correcting these perceptions of Native America and of its centrality to "American" history. He did this as a poet, fiction writer, historian, professor, editor, and publisher. Many years of his life were dedicated to publishing and promoting Native writers through Strawberry Press and his visionary multicultural magazine, *Contact/II*, published for twenty years in New York City, all while hosting countless literary events for Native writers wherever he lived and taught.

In his own writing, Maurice Kenny was especially interested in figures of contact and intersection between Native and European experience: figures such as the Jesuit Missionary, Isaac Jogues, who came to live among the Iroquois and eventually died at their hands; Tekonwatonti/ Molly Brant, the Mohawk leader who married Sir William Johnson and fought with the English against the original American Revolutionaries; and Frida Kahlo whose art and life expressed both Indigenous Mexican and German influences—all of whom bore complex relationships and loyalties in negotiating between white European and Native American culture. In interviews, essays, and personal conversations, Kenny often confessed that he was searching for himself in exploring these historical figures of contact: as a "mixed blood" Mohawk/Irish/Seneca/English, he has expressed strong allegiance to his Native roots while oscillating between acceptance and guilt at being half-European, never fully at home in either culture:

> . . . *like Vine Deloria, as a child, I had rooted for the cowboys and cavalry over the Indians at the Saturday matinee. It was not easy to find myself as half-White, half-Native.*

Monahsetah, Resistance and other Markings on Turtle's Back interrogates that crisis of contact between European-American expansion and the free Cheyenne Nation, and especially the enigmatic woman, Monahsetah, the Cheyenne second "wife" to General George Armstrong Custer, whom the Cheyenne reviled by the sobriquet, "Creeping Panther." In 1868, the warring General Custer captured young Monahsetah after massacring her family and friends on the Washita River, then held her captive as his guide, "translator" and intermediary, until her pregnancy began to show. The relationship between them is still debated by historians, whether Monahsetah was Custer's victim or willing lover, whether she stalled and misled him, aided him reluctantly or was coerced on pain of death into helping Custer's war against the Cheyenne—and whether or not she bore his only child. Maurice Kenny employs multiple camera angles and genres in exploring this history, shifting between points of view and narrative method, from the lyric essay, to poetry, to traditional historical reportage and witness testimony, all with the effect of awakening empathy and imagination, of rendering lived moments within the larger patterns of history. Many of Kenny's poems complement the text, including two long poems that braid through larger prose sections: the poem, "I Am the Sun," written to commemorate the heroes and martyrs of Wounded Knee, builds texture and spiritual resonance within Kenny's treatment of the Sand Creek Massacre; and later, Kenny's "The Dugout" chants through his personal essay, "Betrayal by Memory," as it explores his familial/personal parallels with the Mohawk heroine, Tekonwatonti/Molly Brant.

Maurice Kenny's "mixed blood" heritage remained a source of creative energy during his sixty-year writing career. It could be argued that this dynamic state of betweenness or both-ness, formed the character of the writer, more than any one of his root identities in particular. Fittingly, he chose the title *Between Two Rivers*, ("between two cultures") for the *Selected Works* which gathered the poems from his first several books. In the celebrated poem, "Listening for the Elders," we recognize Kenny's search for Native identity upon his return to Iroquois country after many years in Brooklyn:

> *is summer this bear*
> *home this tamarack*
> *are these wild berries song*
> *is this hill*
> > *where my grandmother sleeps*
> > *this river where*
> > *my father fishes . . .*
>
> *does this woman sing my pain . . .*
>
> *is summer this turtle*
> > *home this sumac*
> > *home this black ash . . .*
> *is summer this story*
> *is summer home*

In tracing Monahsetah's cultural negotiations, Kenny is perhaps, once more, trying to locate himself within that insoluble inquiry: after five centuries of massacre and exploitation, how may one's Native loyalties be reconciled to one's European roots? What forms may resistance take? Who am I and where do I belong? And in this spirit, was Monahsetah loyal to the Cheyenne people or to her white captors? Is it possible to be both? The answers form a Rorschach test for scholars as the historical record provides sufficient data points on all sides of the questions, conflicting witness testimony by often unreliable sources from which a shadow truth must be extrapolated or intuited. Haunted by these questions, Kenny began working on this book in 1966 and only finished it this year as his final literary offering, fifty years later.

I was Maurice Kenny's poetry student at the University of Oklahoma from 1989 to 1992 and remained his lifelong mentee and friend. We crisscrossed the country together giving poetry readings and visiting with Native friends, and I stayed with him in Saranac Lake, NY for two summers where we hiked and kayaked and engaged in hundreds of conversations and debates about Native history and culture and about the art of poetry itself. During his final trip west by Amtrak, I organized a Native American poetry festival in San Francisco to honor him, and I secretly arranged to unite him on stage with his beloved friend, poet Lorna Dee Cervantes, after eighteen years apart. When Maurice asked me to serve as editor to this project, he may not have known how many connections I shared with the story of Custer and Monahsetah. As a mixed blood, myself, with Lakota Sioux on my mother's side and Cherokee on my father's side, it is likely that my Lakota ancestors were involved in Custer's death at the Battle of Little Bighorn. My father, Everett Sweeney—Irish/Cherokee—served as the attorney for the Cheyenne Nation in Oklahoma in the decades-old effort to force the federal government to pay reparations for the atrocities of the Sand Creek Massacre. Growing up, my father and I often attended Cheyenne powwows in Western Oklahoma, where we stomp danced in a circle with the descendants of the heroes of this book—Monahsetah, Little Rock, Black Kettle, White Antelope, Skunk Woman, Little Eagle, Mahwissa, and their Cheyenne brethren. My father taught me to carve and play flutes of Oklahoma red cedar in the Cheyenne style, six holes for the six directions, and we were invited to the Cheyenne Sundance in western Oklahoma by one of Chief Black Kettle's grandsons to observe the powerful initiation rites, three days of dancing through heat, dehydration and spirit vision to the beat of drums until the shapes of the dancers moved in silhouette against the prairie sunset. As a strange play of fate, my father wrote one unpublished novel, entitled

Monahsetah, a detective story which searched for the truth in the Monahsetah legend. In working with Maurice Kenny for the past year, I am grateful for this opportunity to serve the Cheyenne Nation, to collaborate with Dr. Kenny once more and to further our understanding of the same essential mystery that captured my father's attention many years ago, the story of Monahsetah, the Cheyenne woman who changed history.

Maurice Kenny passed away earlier this year during the process of writing this book, the last book that he would write during his prolific career. He was still working on passages and poems exploring the period of 1869 when Monahsetah traveled with Custer as the young general's second wife, guide, and intermediary, helping Custer to track down the remaining Cheyenne who survived the Washita Massacre. This has proven to be the most controversial sequence of the saga, and the most elusive to historians. Kenny was reluctant to "guess" about Monahsetah's level of complicity with Custer and was listening for voices that might explain what truly happened during that time. Kenny's final letter to me expressed that he was in too much pain to sit up at the computer, that he would not write any more for the book. It is likely that the last poem he wrote in his lifetime is "Monahsetah's Answer," which reveals his anxiety about being an intruder to Monahsetah's story—"hey you half breed, white man with blue eyes,"—as well as his concerns about misreading her motives, victimizing her all over again by getting the story wrong. Through painstaking research he sought to be as accurate to fact as possible, but he also knew that the historical record had limits for which imagination, channeling or, what he called, "listening" were required to restore those scenes that history could not bring back in the flesh. Sometimes history needs a poet. The resulting work is a braiding of history and intuition, poetry and memoir, into what we could call *lyric history*.

As this is the last book that Maurice Kenny wrote, he wanted some of his poems and personal essays to appear alongside the epic of Monahsetah. This collage of history, memoir, poems, and even recipes, is working to bridge psychic landscapes and thematic terrain that have not only defined his own life, but have described the traceries of European and Native conflict and exchange. When I interviewed Maurice Kenny for *World Literature Today* a few years ago, he recognized that his writing about Frida Kahlo, Tekonwatonti, and Monahsetah all included personal inquiries in search of the Self, of mother and father, of origin and identity. At one point while sitting in his living room in Potsdam, New York, Kenny broke into tears at this realization, especially that he was reliving his quest for mother and father again and again. The final essay in the book, "Betrayal by Memory: Tekonwatonti/Molly Brant," takes a deeper look at some of his familial and psychological links to the powerful Mohawk woman, Tekonwatonti, and her Irish husband, Sir William Johnson. In the brief essay, "On Turtle's Back," Kenny comes to interpret the apparently random objects in his house as artifacts, symbols, and markers of meaningful experiences all over America, of the interconnectedness of stories linking the mundane to divine, ancient patterns across the sacred Iroquois Turtle's back; this investigation of the "knick-knacks" in his living room further serves as metaphor for how history is puzzled together from remnants, how the markers that remain form maps to the past, if we only know how to read them.

Lastly, it was important to Maurice Kenny that we not mistake the atrocities against the Cheyenne as isolated incidents limited to the domain of the past, as the story of Monahsetah is the story of Native people up and down both American continents and persists to this day, where conditions of poverty, underfunded education, health, indignity, and unemployment are pandemic, where Native Americans wield little political power and harmful stereotypes persist, where new oil pipelines join train tracks, interstates and cattle fences in defiling and segmenting Native land.

> *While living in contemporary Mexico, again I was made aware of the "Indian situation" up and down two continents composing this hemisphere. A rampant racism so prevalent across these beautiful lands: poverty, poor housing in hovels squatting next to churches built in gold on Indian backs . . ."*

We remember the past to restore the present, and the story of every sage smoke and every wolf pup is our own story. As Kenny's poem "The Dugout" powerfully expresses, we are born into this great story which includes Monahsetah, the Love of Maheo which surrounds us and holds us up, our Mother in "the berry on the bramble," and the fall of Sky Woman which began our human saga. This is also the story of how Maurice Kenny, a Mohawk/Irishman, came to be who he was, to commit to a lifetime of service, art, community, and exploration, and how we are connected by Story across the decades and across the miles by the patterns on Turtle's Back.

—Chad Sweeney
December 2016

For those who fell in all the wars . . .
especially at Sand Creek and at the Washita

And in memory of Mary Dickson
who spent a harrowing night at the Creek,
and the winds which swirl the dust to this
very moment

And in memory
Diane Decorah
Diane Burns
Peter Blue cloud

BOOK I

MONAHSETAH: A STORY OF RESISTANCE

Monahsehtah

Evicted into the frozen teeth of winter
by the landlords of the plains;
cast into the bloody waters of the Washita
where your father's corpse flowed in the stream . . .
his manhood stuffed into his mouth,
his scalp made guidon for Custer's soldiers.
Torn from the band of helpless captive women,
a suckling child, mewing and puking in your arms;
driven by Long Hair to feel out the ashes of the village,
scout out the vital hearts of your people.

Did Sheridan's eyes admire the loveliness
of your young Cheyenne cheeks?
Did Custer claim you like a trophy until
his civil wife pulled his sweaty thighs
from the Cheyenne Mystery of your life?!
You held your childish hands to your womb
and felt the kickings of a bird, the fledgling seed
planted like so much corn by Yellow-locked Long Hair!
Where did you find the love to mount his cot, knifeless,
or did he find your flesh upon his earthen floor?!

Custer strutted your grave to glory, foolish girl.
Now in the winds of the Washita Valley cottonwoods cry
for the slain Cheyenne. No winds moan in the leaves
for the head-strong girl, daughter of Little Rock,
who followed the pony soldiers.

Monahsetah's Answer

How do I answer?

Do I call, hey you half breed, white man
with blue eyes, you half red man standing
within your breech clout?
                                        You ask why
did I not take my knife and rush it
into his belly allowing his enemy blood
to river into my people's Oklahoma earth.

He called me to his bed.
His tent would be my sacrificial altar.
His body become my demise once my face
had been softly stroked by his hand . . . cold,
clammy; his body. I was his war treasure,
a hunk of gold, a pot of flesh. There was no escape.

In fact his man took my knife and slit an open
run of blood on my arm . . . just to warn
that I had better smile and be content.

Monahsetah's Early Life
And a Personal Renaissance

1966

In the winter of 1966 I returned from living several years in Mexico, Puerto Rico, then St. Thomas in the Virgin Islands.

> *The morning rained*
> *but pavements and tables dried*
> *easily under Zapotec suns*
> *Comfortable with coke and frijoles . . .*
> *I held wind-thoughts of nothing,*
> *or thought only of old Indians selling corn gods*

I was sitting in Chicago O'Hare airport reading Mari Sandoz' Cheyenne Autumn, three years before a takeover of Alcatraz Island by Native people, and seven years before the Wounded Knee occupation in South Dakota on the Lakota reservation at Pine Ridge.

On my return I began to see America, as did many others, in a truer light than I had ever before had the courage to see it.

Barbra Streisand was the reigning queen of song and was starring in *Funny Girl* on Broadway. The horrors of Vietnam showed nightly on the 7 o'clock news. American streets were burning. Anger in those streets was justified. American troops were on the soil of a country to which they had no right. Indigenous people in thatched villages were being murdered, napalmed.

It took courage to truly observe the land of my birth where part of my blood was hated and the other part imported into a land knee-deep in genocide and bloody with racism, sexism and homophobia, blockades to liberty and happiness let alone sexual fulfillment.

In the U.S., a fight for freedom, equality and civil rights was fought in nearly every town in the country, especially those southern towns which denied humanity to human beings. Despite this new attention to race in America, Native Americans were still invisible, totally ignored.

1860

Monahsetah, sometimes known as Me-o-tzi, happily played games along the creeks and streams with the other children of the village. She played stickball with her friends, but sometimes when others wanted to play tipi-living, she refused. She calmly looked about, not finding a boy with whom she would want to build a stick lodge, she sulked, and wandered down the creek bed looking for wildflowers or berries to bring her mother, or pretty pebbles, a gift for her father, Ho-han-i-no-o.

Once in a shallow stream she found a small rough stone that when held to the sun flickered with tiny lights. She brought this to her father. The gift pleased him so much that he tied it around his neck and told her it would forever be part of his war medicine.

His name was Little Rock. It was fitting that he should carry her stone of lights about his throat. It would be his symbol. He would drop the weight of his powers upon their enemies as the stone would drop through pools of the stream, straight through the heart of the waters, straight to the enemy's heart.

This pleased the girl and encouraged her search for bright stones, but never again did she find a nugget as shiny and beautiful as the one hanging from her father's neck. It became a game; wherever the band traveled she would search the streams.

Monahsetah, though greatly alone by her own choice, was a cheerful child. She composed songs to sing when the family gathered about the night fires. Every object impelled song:

> a magpie in flight,
> shadow of a willow,
> the shape of rolling
> clouds, the color
> of ponies grazing in a meadow

While gathering grains or roots for the stew pot she would often discover ants or other insects gathering their foods, and she would compose a song of the harvesters. She would sing of the buffalo, the hunt and kill, and his stripped bones drying white in the burning sun; or she would sing of a pet dog, old and handicapped, throttled by her mother and dropped into the pot.

Normally a happy child, Monahsetah sang spontaneous songs and prayers of thanks for all living things the Great Spirit had given her people.

1966

Latinos were relegated to the kitchen and Asian-Americans were swept into the laundry room. Black was beautiful to some places and peoples of America and not so much in other places. The climate wasn't pretty, and we should never forget the pain and suffering here in this land of opportunity, the great and magnificent land of plenty for ALL.

Tourists and markets behind . . . no need
for cheap ornaments that keep
Indians alive, lazy and without revolution.

This "Indian," of course, was myself lazing in Mexico and on Caribbean beaches.

What wind thoughts blew the six years;
what Indian sold my mementos . . .
what angry and silly-faced gods!
Across Sheridan Square the wind blows the mind.
I wonder what revelation, which revolution.

. . .

I quiver with the excitement of anticipation
and walk east and north toward 14th Street.

I had awakened and was attempting to declare war on inhumanity, the murder of all innocent peoples of both past and present.

Not involved with any organization, platform or slogan, I did somehow devise the idea that the counter-culture in New York City lived and fermented on Manhattan's Lower East Side, or at least the poets lived there among the squalor of that slum. Hence my idea of walking east and north out of Sheridan Square, symbolically joining those, in Norman Mailer's term, *armies of the night*.

However, my fervor was cast into a more poetic mold than that of bearing physical or verbal arms, neither pacification nor actual confrontation such as at Wounded Knee. Age most likely had something to do with that decision. I was certainly not the youthful hippie with long golden hair whose chest bounced a necklace of the peace symbol, nor was I to become a member of A.I.M. which had not yet been organized.

1860

Yet all was not play and song for Monahsetah. Her mother, grandmother and aunts taught her "women's duties" of lodge and field: how to pitch a lodge, to follow hunters and skin the kill, how to prepare hide for clothing, moccasins and lodge skins.

Her mother taught her the rudiments of pounding pemmican—dried buffalo meat, berries and animal fat mixed and stuffed into guts like sausage—which helped hold the band over those fierce and hungry winters when fresh game was not available. The girl was taught to dry the buffalo meat for jerky, how to start a fire, and how to keep coals alive in dung once the village packed and was on the move. She was taught to sew and cook and gather.

She was expected to learn various ceremonial prayers to insure fertility of roots and berries, animals and humans; the prayers and songs of traditional rituals and social organizations. There was much for a little girl to learn and remember, a robust and complete education.

Yet unlike other girls of her age in the village, Monahsetah was not quite so willing or eager to accept the life of a common woman, the drudgery and slavery to lodge and husband.

She was the daughter of *Ho-han-i-no-o* (Little Rock), second chief to the band that followed *Moke-to-ve-to* (Black Kettle) across the plains and streams at the feet of the *Wah-to-yah* (Spanish Peaks). Surely she was meant to be the proud wife of a great and victorious chief, the first wife, a woman not meant to spend her summers scavenging for buffalo chips to feed the cook fires. Surely she was not meant to waste her youth and intelligence in pounding pemmican and chewing hide for moccasins.

As a very small girl she had often been in position to listen at important council meetings; she observed the pride and dignity of various chiefs; she watched her own father and others strut about the council lodge arguing, persuading, cajoling the others to his thoughts and desires. She nestled within the folds of her blankets, breathing the acrid scents of the rising smoke of the Sacred Pipe, the Holy Sweetgrass or burning Sage. She listened to White Antelope, to Black Kettle and Roman Nose.

If her beauty alone did not command respect and protect her from drudgery, then surely her blood and intelligence would demand a better life than that which would be portioned the other girls of the village.

1966

I was angry by everything wrong with America, past and present, yet I did not want to join some army or other. All my life I had been aware of injustice, and aware of lies and inaccuracies of the official history of this country. I fully realized that if there was an "oppressed," then there was definitely an "oppressor."

Yet, like Vine Deloria, as a child, I had rooted for the cowboys and cavalry over the Indians at the Saturday matinee. It was not easy to find myself as half-White, half-Native.

While living in contemporary Mexico, again I was made aware of the "Indian situation" up and down two continents composing this hemisphere. A rampant racism so prevalent across these beautiful lands: poverty, poor housing in hovels squatting next to churches built in gold on Indian backs—

and a program of extermination of Indians and their alternate way of life through whatever means, and especially amalgamation, assimilation, of those same Indians, relocation into major cities, both in Latin America and the United States where governments encouraged the Indian to disappear, cleanly disposed—

or in the old cavalry term, *dispatched.*

Historians agree that the European-Americans of the 18th and 19th centuries firmly believed in their rights and privileges to all Native American lands.

This was already an old idea and justification for policy before Washington commanded his revolutionary forces and before Franklin copied the Constitution of the U.S. from the Iroquois Confederacy, the Great League, and the Great Law of Peace freely binding these Nations together, forming the strongest alliance known on the continent, a formidable strength that worried the English, French, Spanish and Colonial Americans alike.

Attitudes and policies of *manifest destiny* and *material progress* were already old before Jefferson concluded the Louisiana Purchase and sent the Lewis and Clark expedition into the corner of the far northwest. The Europeans left their home continent because of dire impoverishment and religious persecution. The Puritan Pilgrims never entertained the thought of returning to their native shores, not even before they discovered the vast natural riches of this American continent.

As Stephen E. Ambrose argues in *Crazy Horse and Custer*:

> *They have believed in that doctrine more than in their Constitution or their treaties, or their religion. America's leaders and America's white population have allowed nothing to stand in the path of progress. Not a tree, nor a desert, not a river, nothing. Most certainly not Indians, regrettable as it may have been to have to destroy such noble and romantic people.*

Indians were, and remain, the enemies of that progress.

For every white hair the Indian plucked from the red chin of the plains a dozen sprouted as replacement.

1863

Often in late spring, off gathering berries in the long dew-wet grass of early morning, Monahsetah would wander off by herself and allow childish dreams to envelop her senses and spirit.

Monahsetah imagined herself married to a handsome Brave who truly loved her.

He would take many ponies from enemies, Pawnee or Ute, and make them rich. They would give large feasts and hold giveaways, sharing their bounty, and would be envied by all the band. And he would recognize her personal strength.

Perhaps she would even advise her husband on tribal policy when he earned followers and was made a chief.

Had not *Ho-han-i-no-o*, her own father, shown the girl the way to wisdom and fed her with the food of intelligence. Her summers and winters would be crowded with joy and pleasure and the respect of her people; she would grow old softly, gently, and as a grandmother would teach her sons to be great hunters, warriors, great chiefs, great *Tsististas*; and her daughters would be prepared to be the finest women of the Nation, the *Wi-ta-pi-u*.

Her daydreams would cast such heavy spells that often the other girls gathering berries nearby would call out and ask were she sleeping, and tease that her berries had rotted in the basket.

1966

I returned to the U.S. determined to put whatever power as a writer and as a human being and as an Iroquois I had to work for the people, and all peoples; to shed some truth, offer fresh insight upon official history(s); and to help make history(s) accurate, a possible measure for the future of all peoples oppressed and hungry.

My re-entry to America was a second birth as a human being, a Native person and a writer. I was sitting in Chicago O'Hare airport reading Mari Sandoz' classic history, *Cheyenne Autumn*, detailing the betrayal and destruction of the Cheyenne nation at the lance of the U.S. military. I heard Monahsetah speak to me from within this tragic sequence of events, and I promised to look for her among the bones and flags of history.

Mari Sandoz proved one flashlight beam that I held in my hands, and her writing shed a solid ray of light onto some of those historic lies.

My work to shine a light toward Monahsetah is a simple beginning. With such friends and associates I shall take my study further into the dark but important depths of history to help correct inaccuracies and to explore those quieter human moments as well as the felt truth of actually being there during those infamous wars/massacres. Hopefully this is one more flashlight shedding one more ray onto the noble and beautiful people of the plains.

It is difficult to explain, but I felt a kinship with Monahsetah and her struggle. At age 20, she was allegedly forced to the ground by Major General George Armstrong Custer after his dawn attack of her people on the Washita River in the present state of Oklahoma.

Creeping Panther, as Custer was commonly known by the Cheyenne, kept the young woman as his translator until her womb began to round with new life. Was Monahsetah a slave or lover, victim or wife—or all of these in one way or another? Did Custer know that she already had a baby with her at the Washita? Did he knowingly separate her from this child?

Creeping Panther kept her as his "translator" though she could speak no English and he could speak no Cheyenne. For six months, Monahsetah traveled with Custer, sleeping in his tent. She is accused of being a traitor to her people, of sleeping with the enemy, and of even going so far as to serve as guide to Custer while he hunted down the Cheyenne who had escaped from the Washita Massacre.

It is argued that Custer's European-American *veho* wife, Elizabeth, pressured Custer to release Monahsetah before their child was born, or that Custer hurriedly sent Monahsetah away to avoid scandal, to be removed from the plains and relocated with the other surviving Cheyenne.

What is beyond all doubt is that Monahsetah was a remarkable human being, and her story of resilience, resistance, adaptation and survival is the story of Native America. In 1966, I began looking for her, and somewhere along the way, I found myself.

Legend

Monahsetah went into story
long tales and short talks
probably imagined,
perhaps a handful true
to few facts of her breath

or "poor" Custer, what did
happen to your body . . .
some say Crazy Horse shot
an arrow thru your heart . . .
others demand that
Rain-in-the-Face ate
your heart raw
without a pinch of salt . . .
others believe your own
soldiers shot you in the back
and you slipped off your pony
into the waters of that
Little Big Horn to await
Elizabeth's return
to clean your name
from a muddy slate

Monahsetah grew into story with
one boy child, Yellow Swallow,
ghost child partially erased
by Elizabeth's many pens

1863

Many winters before as a little girl, Monahsetah's father, Little Rock, had taken her to the adobe village of Bent's Fort, and the girl saw with her own amazed eyes the faces and slim figures of the *veho* women. She stared at their pretty, colorful frocks, their comparative material wealth.

Now as a young maiden she remembered. Perhaps if a *veho* were to see her, recognize her own prettiness, he would take her to live in Bent's Fort where she could dress in the fine costumes that their women wore. They seemed to have the advantages of one type of freedom, yet they seemed stiff as well, as if the control exerted upon them came from within themselves rather than from their men and elders. Their world was beautiful, but it must have contained its own types of drudgery. There seemed many ways to be a woman.

Dresses of blue and pink with skirts billowing with the wind around their thin ankles; these dresses topped with bright hats plumed with long and gay feathers of strange birds. Would she ever wear slippers of shiny black leather laced to the calf of her leg? Would she carry the thing they called a "parasol" so the sun would not hurt her eyes?

Monahsetah was stubborn and determined, and her determination was not viewed as natural. Few women objected to their lives and knew their importance to their husbands, children and certainly to their village and Nation. Yet she had heard of women so unhappy with their lot in life that they would wander off and either marry a *veho* (white man) or hang themselves from a chinaberry tree.

This, too, was unnatural, a waste of the gifts of the Great Spirit, and a tragic stain upon the band.

Monahsetah heard the stories, rumors, of these women who so vigorously rejected what they considered to be an abject state that suicide was preferred. She also heard the gossip of the older women of the village saying it wasn't any better living with a *veho* in his fort or trapper's camp. *Vehos* were known to beat their women, hand them around on the plains, make them drunkards, and often worked them harder than a Cheyenne husband would.

She decided she would never take her own life, never put a leather thong about her own neck. That was wrong; her body had its own spirit that wanted life. And she doubted she would like marriage with a *veho* who always carried the sweet stink, had briars on his chin and was known to whip his Indian wife and throw her out of the lodge when he was sick and crazy on whiskey.

There were a number of these "grey" men in her village and she had watched how they treated their wives. They were not all gentle nor as kind as Trader Bent, the one called the Little White Man, who had married Owl Woman.

And she remembered how ridiculous she would look wearing *veho* clothing—

for she remembered the day a party of warriors had returned to the village from a raid dressed in all that colorful finery that *veho* women wore. They looked silly and ugly as they whooped through the camp. One brave had tossed a feather boa around his neck and the sticky little feathers were blowing into his face, his eyes and mouth—they blinded him and his horse led him right into a lodge!

It was fun, perhaps, dressing in these *veho* costumes, but not practical. It made you the laughingstock of the camp. Even thinking about marriage to a *veho* was indeed wild dreaming. It was not good to dream such things. The other girls would laugh and tease her; her mother would scold if she were to know what seeds sprang to life in her thoughts. Her father would be angry, he would marry her immediately to a Cheyenne Brave. It was not Cheyenne to allow this ridiculous nonsense to rule her intelligence.

Regardless, she would not be a slave to drudgery.

1864

One night as the campfires leaped nearly as high as the lodge poles, an old man rode a white horse through the village calling for all to listen. Monahsetah put down the moccasin which she had been sewing and stepped to the lodge entrance. The old man cried that a girl was to be married, a young girl who had been her friend.

Monahsetah stepped out into the calm summer evening and the shaking lights of glowing fires. Her dark skin reflected the crimson and orange flames. As she stood in the shadows of the village streets, she recalled the thin figure of her friend . . . a dull, cowering girl, not pretty or terribly bright, but she would make her Brave a good wife.

She remembered the ceremony. The grandmother had undressed the childlike figure and daubed vermillion to her naked body until her skin screamed red.

The old woman placed a buffalo robe about the girl
and led her to a smudge fire of sagebrush. The fire
was so small
it could have been held
in the hand. The girl stood naked and cold
above the burning sage. The smoke bathed
her frightened flesh. The small milky tongues,
pungent and scared, reached out to touch her ankles
and slipped to her calves and knees, lapping along her thighs,
crept slowly along her belly and tiny breasts
that blossomed like mountain plums
still clinging to the branch.

The grandmother held the fur robe about her.

The smoke wafted along her arms, bathed her face and brought tears to stinging eyes. When the child's body had been thoroughly washed with the cleansing, purifying smoke of the holy sage, she was dressed and carried off to stay in a lodge where she would be given no fresh meat to eat.

Four days she remained excluded from the people of the village. Her grandmother stayed near to protect her solitude and ensure her purity. At the end of the four days the grandmother passed a rope around the girl's waist and between her thighs. Only then, as a maiden, did she re-enter village life and enter a new adulthood.

Tonight, thought Monahsetah, her Brave would untie that rope and in the *Tsististas* way they would be securely married in conjugal union. In the moon of falling leaves she would bear a child, a warrior for her people.

Monahsetah could not help think that one day in the very imminent and frightening future she, too, would be readied by her own grandmother to stand above the holy sage in a sacred manner, the sage burning and purging all evil, purifying her blood and her flesh so that future Cheyenne generations would remain untainted, assured of survival.

She contemplated how she would stand waiting for the knobby old hands to tie away her new womanhood to protect it from a curious boy who might bring disgrace upon her and upon the Cheyenne.

She shuddered and stooped to enter the lodge again. She would not attend the marriage ceremony of her friend.

1970

In 1970, Dee Brown's massive compendium, *Bury My Heart at Wounded Knee*, broke records on the *New York Times* book list. No doubt an important history, but another account focused on military tactics, war, blood and death, the deaths of many great Nations and the slaughter of a people struggling to survive under the onslaught of the industrial revolution and European-American conquest. Despite Brown's deep and abiding sympathy for Native people, he made little effort to represent Native resilience, nor other strengths beyond that of the Warrior. Placing the book down upon completion one would think that the Native peoples of this land had been totally wiped out, vanquished and vanished.

Brown failed to present the entire spectrum, to explore and celebrate the total circumference of life and culture. He rarely hints at the great Six Nation League, the Iroquois Confederacy, nor the essential spirituality of these Native Nations across the lands, the incredible arts created by Native artisans and craftsman, the Native will to survive and the cost of that survival.

Moccasin

Listen . . .
moccasin moccasin
            circle circle
            dance dance

    drums drum
            pound pound
    rattles rattle
            sing sing

    wind howls like a wolf on the hill

thunders thunder
      shake shake

wind sings in the cold air

moccasin moccasin
      move move

wind howls
wind sings
      leaves fall in the frost
      apples ripen in the frost
      wolves seek lairs in the frost
      snow falls
      hills rise
      sun sets
        sun sun
          sets

moccasin moccasin

      circle circle
      dance dance

we come to greet and thank
      the winds
      the birds
      the snow
      the drum
      the drummer
      the dance
      the dancer
    move move
    sun move
    moccasin

1864

Nights grew colder and the women made larger fires in the lodges. Fires were kept burning in the meadows for the pony herders, and other fires burned in the low hills to ward off stray packs of hungry wolves prowling the darkness at the edge of the herds and the edge of the village. Strong winds rushed across the plains from *Wah-to-yah*, the two great mountains named Two Breasts of Earth.

The Cheyenne were warm in their tipis but hungry. The summer hunt had not been plentiful, and the women could not prepare sufficient pemmican or jerky to hold the band over the months of heavy snows and cold now that game was settled into seclusion for winter.

More *veho* wagons rolled across the open plains and out dropped *ki-kuns* (children) who shot up overnight to pitch log cabins or earthen lodges. They cut the cottonwoods and willows and burnt the buffalo grasses.

Buffalo (*pte*) disliked the smells of the *vehos* and shied away from their camps, trailed further and further off from the Indian villages as well. *Pte* dropped to the fire-sticks of the *vehos* or to Ute arrows, but the Cheyenne seldom found *pte* on the open prairie near their villages.

The buffalo was slowly forsaking his brothers, and falling to the enemy.

It must be that *pte* was angry with his red brothers for letting the *vehos* dig the earth with the sticks that trailed the horse and to separate the plains with the wheels of their wagons and the trails of their iron-horse that stopped and turned *pte* about. He would not cross the iron road . . . its smell was bad, dangerous.

Buffalo and the deer and antelope, were disappearing and left the Cheyenne pots empty or with little more than scavenged roots or an old dog too sick and weary to pull a travois further down the trail.

Sometimes the steaming pots would contain the bones and flesh of the *vehos'* buffalo, called "cattle." Its meat remained always second choice. It was tough and stringy and not of the earth. Yet the beef kept the voice of the stomach quiet; it stilled the hungry cries of the children.

Often young men of the band would leave the village in small hunting parties and return a few days later with these scrawny cows, whooping into camp that there was now food for all.

There was a sadness on the faces of these young men, and no real pride in their accomplishments. For a short time no pot would be empty and no sorrowful cry in the lodges. Then, slowly the shrunken stomachs emptied and cried in anger.

The young hunters would ride out
again, but return
with cows—cows
rather than buffalo
or deer—
tails
whisking behind, eyes
rolling
in their heads.

Even in winter there were many visitors in the village: traders, scouts, bluecoats of the long knives, agents. William Bent came to the lodge of his new wife, Yellow Woman, sister to the dead Owl Woman, and his three sons and two daughters were constantly in and out of camp.

"Uncle" John Smith with his half-Cheyenne son, Jack Smith, was often seen trading in Black Kettle's or War Bonnet's lodges. Monahsetah once saw the white-black man, Jim Buckworth, Medicine Calf, toothless and scraggly. She thought he should go to the hills and sing his death song. He was old and smelled of whiskey and his mulatto skin was tanned and tough as a buffalo hide. She knew he had lived with the Crow many winters.

She heard "Uncle" John whisper that old Medicine Calf was like a Crow, a dirty thief.

William Bent was white, a *veho*, but she could feel his understanding and affection as if he was more Cheyenne. Monahsetah knew he respected the people because he brought them food, and some whiskey, and spoke to the pony soldiers that Black Kettle's band was not hostile and wanted only peace with the whites and to return to the old ways.

She had played all her life with the Bent children and knew them as cousins. When their father sent them east to school she sincerely missed them. When they returned they scratched signs in the dust of the ground and called these symbols *words*.

His son, George, had become educated sufficiently to write letters to the government for Black Kettle. Charlie, the youngest boy, wasn't quite as nice a boy as George or Robert. He teased her, accusing her of wanting to color her blood. He taunted how he had seen her watch the white man, especially the pony soldiers, and that one day she would walk into their camp.

Monahsetah protested, and threw dirt in Charley's face. It was not good nor wise for him to talk this foolishness, dangerous, especially for the daughter of Little Rock who was suspicious toward whites. Her father did not trust these men of pale flesh, light hair and split tongue. For the next few weeks, she allowed Little Eagle and other Cheyenne men to flirt with her. She let herself be seen walking with them or lingering too long outside the tipi, but she remained proud and dignified and did not let any of them get too close.

It was not Cheyenne to lie, but she had to admit that the *veho* pony soldiers held a strange fascination. She enjoyed listening to their difficult speech. They talked in a lazy manner or as though they were ill with fever, never sharp and pointed like the Cheyenne. She didn't know what they were saying, but she intuited that they were confident, as if the future belonged to them.

Monahsetah resolved never to walk into an adobe village, nor would she ever share her robe with a *veho*. He stank of whiskey and was known to beat Indian wives. Charley Bent was wrong, completely wrong. She did not wish to color her blood, to water it down with a *veho*.

He teased her only because he was half white and ashamed.

One morning a great agitation came over the village. Bear Tongue, a mounted crier, rode through the streets calling out to the people that pony soldiers approached; that their lines stood tall and wide. Warriors ran to the lodge, dressed and painted as if for war. They assembled the horses and weapons in the event of an attack. Fear and anger boiled in their hearts. Mounted in line they awaited the pony chiefs whose horses slowly trotted to the village edge.

Monahsetah slipped from her lodge and went to stare at the bluecoats. Her heart tightened at the thought of an attack, and sought her father who comforted her fears by saying it was Major Wynkoop whom they called Tall Chief from Fort Lyon. Though Tall Chief was possibly the only friend the *Tsististas* had in the bluecoats' lodge, she should still prepare herself to flee with the helpless ones should guns be fired.

Monahsetah drew as close as she dared to the opposing lines of chiefs, warriors and soldiers to get a good sight on this white man, Tall Chief. She observed him signal to Black Kettle that he was there on a peaceful mission. Black Kettle approached, held the hand of Tall Chief, and then, with One Eye, White Antelope, Little Raven of the Arapaho, and others, went to the war lodge to smoke and talk. Though merely a teenage girl, Monahsetah, followed closely at her father's heel, and entered under the flap of the tipi silently hoping no one would object to her being there.

She looked closely at the bluecoat named Tall Chief. There was *veho's* smoke between his teeth, the paper brown and wet, curls and puffs of smoke rising in the air.

She had seen this man before. He always carried this smoke in his mouth. Medicine to keep bad spirits away? He was not ugly for a bluecoat, but his little mustache needed trimming and his uniform was baggy. He was long as a lodge pole and thin as a sapling. His back was slightly rounded and the hairs of his head were dying. It must be that he was sick.

All *vehos* looked sick, and, indeed, had brought much illness to her people and all the peoples of her known world. The shrinking and coughing disease.

Whole villages had taken to the run and died; many children left with great holes in their faces.

She shivered, wondered if Tall Chief had the burning sickness under his bluecoat. This man was not unfriendly though he was firm in his talk. This morning he had brought sugar for the children and bags of coffee for the chiefs who accepted his presents gratefully.

This Tall Chief spoke long with Black Kettle and the other leaders. John Smith and young George Bent interpreted.

One Eye stepped through the tight circle of chiefs and asked to speak. Some of the leaders did not want him to waste words as he was only a sub-chief, and not only a peace chief but a great lover of *vehos*.

First One Eye took up a pipe and then calmly, respectively, addressed the assembled chiefs, quietly and briefly. He told of his having risked his life to deliver the letter George Bent wrote to the bluecoats for Black Kettle. He spoke, sighting his faith and belief in not only the honesty of the Cheyenne, his people, but in their peaceful intentions.

One Eye knew the Cheyenne tongue did not split, and that their pledge to peace must hold.

He relayed that he had promised the pony soldier chief that he would not paint for war and he meant to keep to that promise. If need be he would sing his death song before the arrows of his people, the *Tsististas*, or before the bluecoats' spitting rifles.

Looking at the faces gathered in the lodge, One Eye announced to all that he would cross to the side of the whites if his people did not honor this pledge. He threatened that many of his friends would follow him to the pony soldiers' lodge.

Strong disagreement in the form of distressed grumbles rose from among the ranks after One Eye's speech.

Left Hand, chief to the Arapaho, spoke.

Then Little Raven spoke.

Though both chiefs had raided white settlements, run off horses and cows from the farms, and had been known to take the warpath, they favored peace with the bluecoats.

Hidden in the shadows of the smoky council lodge, Monahsetah could remember having seen captives about the village, young women and children loaned or sold to various Braves.

She watched the face of Black Kettle for signs of either anger or conciliation. He betrayed neither. The calm, dignified face told nothing of what burned in his heart or rankled in his mind, the anxiety, fear and hope or the turmoil that as head chief of the *Wi-ta-pi-u* band must coil like serpents in the very center of his being, tying and knotting his brain.

Black Kettle, *Moke-to-ve-to*, the aging peace chief, sat silently, his right hand clasped the wrinkling skin of his left.

No feather hung
in Black Kettle's hair, nor paint
stained
his cheeks. His braids,
rolled in beaver skin, hung down
his chest, and a blanket pulled
about his waist. Pensive
though resilient,
wise not exclamatory,
quiet not negative,
this proud man held
his words,
weighed them,
as each man in the lodge
thundered and roared,
demanded and threatened.

Black Kettle slowly gathered his thoughts, preparing to offer advice. He would not shout commands, nor barter thin sentiments like children, he would not waste breath as he would not waste the meat of *pte* nor the life of a single child or rabbit; he would neither humiliate nor ingratiate himself, for that was not the way of the Cheyenne.

The writhing light
of the lodge fire
rose and bathed the chief's face,
painted shadows on his brow
across the cheeks. The lights
flared upwards along the deerskin shirt and
gathered him within the glow.
The orange and red light pulsed
against the firm, resolute chin,
and as if someone
passed between
Black Kettle's figure and the fire,
the glow was suddenly exterminated
and the chief was plunged into darkness.

The young girl,
Monahsetah,
spying
in the shadows, grew terrified.

The fire writhed
against Black Kettle's face, and now
this darkness completely blocked him from view.

Seemingly immobile, a thin somewhat comforting smile slightly parted Black Kettle's adamant mouth. His thoughts in one hand, his hope and wishes in the other, he weighed all. He possessed resolution; a knowledge of what he must do. Gathering the folds of his blanket about him, clutched to the waist in one hand, he rose and spoke softly to the anxious men sitting about the fire of the lodge.

He spoke in his belief in the white man's honesty,
that the troubles with the white man were over.

He meant to follow the advice of the Tall Chief, Major Wynkoop, who had spoken in friendship and understanding to the *Wi-ta-pi-u.*

Black Kettle told Tall Chief that his people were hungry and that it was difficult to persuade an angry belly. He admitted that some of his young Braves painted for the raiding party even though he had attempted to hold them back, as he believed most of these depredations were the results of the white man's own actions.

Too many whites were crowding the banks of the Platte
and the Arkansas, the Canadian.
They had burnt off the lands, cut down
the cottonwoods, driven off the buffalo,
and slaughtered his children.

He spoke of the braves who had retaliated, who had taken captives that were held in the camps along the river. He felt that before the captives could be released, peace between all brothers must be tightly tied and honestly assured. He would advise his brothers to turn the captives over to the pony soldiers, the whites, but that he could not force the return. In the Cheyenne Nation, laws and rules were made by all—never by a single chief.

With these words the council ended and Tall Chief and his soldiers rode out of the village.

On the following day as the sun reached the center of the sky, Black Kettle appeared at the edge of the pony soldiers' camp and released the white captives held in his village.

With these many comings and goings the encampment was busy and somewhat festive as the visitors often brought presents of both food and trinkets. As the days shortened the nights grew long and as the nights lengthened, they grew colder. Finally snow settled upon the village of Black Kettle's *Wi-ta-pi-u*.

While gathering dried seeds one morning, Monahsetah noticed a party of chiefs ride out of the village. Black Kettle was dressed and painted for war. His long braids, wrapped in beaver skins, hung down his proud chest; even the tail of his pony was rolled and tied. His white deer-skin shirt shone brightly in the morning sunlight; his blanket had been tied about his waist with one point trailing the flanks of his pony. He wore a single feather at the back of his head, but the chief carried no lance nor shield, nor bow and quiver of arrows. He had no weapons with him at all.

She watched the men, Neva, an Arapaho, and White Wolf of the Kiowa, also dressed for a war party. One Eye and White Antelope and Bull Bear cantered up to join the others.

Mostly old men, they were handsome in their beautiful paints astride their ponies, a few which were painted with jags of lightning or spoked suns. John Smith and his sullen half-breed son, Jack, rode with the chiefs. *Na-to-mah*, Jack's mother, waved them off.

The women of the village sang strong heart songs of encouragement.

Monahsetah wondered why these chiefs were dressed and painted for war and what path they were to follow as they chanted their war songs. Surely this was not a raiding party; they were mostly old men. Black Kettle was a peace chief; he hadn't been on the warpath or in a raiding party for a long time. Besides, these warriors carried no visible weapons.

One Eye turned in the saddle, faced the village, and cried out that it was a good day to die.

Monahsetah picked up her grass basket and went in search of her father.

Little Rock explained that the chiefs had gone to the *vehos'* war lodge in Denver, and would parley there with the white chiefs for peace. They would ask to be allowed to remain in this their father's land; and to ask for provisions of food and supplies to hold them over a strong winter that gathered in the western mountains.

Many sleeps later the chiefs returned, stone-faced and silent. They held counsels with all of the chiefs of the bands present in that encampment. Through long hours of the chilling night, many pipes were smoked.

It was decided among the chiefs that the village would move to a new camp on *Ponoeohe*, Sand Creek. The village was to be pitched forty miles above Bent's Ranch and Fort Lyon where the pony soldiers' lodge and Tall Chief Wynkoop offered the people protection.

When Monahsetah asked her father who the soldiers were protecting the people from, he could only shake his head that he did not know.

Little Rock rose from the fire,
weary and worried, walked
to a nearby knoll,
facing the east, prayed to *Maheo*, the Great Spirit
the Everywhere Spirit who had given the people
breath in the morning and sleep at night,
who gave them the buffalo and the rivers,
who gave them mothers for their children
and strong warriors; and who gave them wise chiefs
to lead the *Tsististas* over the plains
in search of food
and safety through the hills.

He prayed to mother earth,
and to the four winds and to the rains,
and he offered prayer to the swiftness of the arrow
and also to the tobacco in the pouch dangling at his side.

He prayed to the winds, the stars, to grandmother moon and father sun.

The village prepared to move to Sand Creek.
Monahsetah helped dismantle the family lodge.

In a few sleeps once again the village tipis stood tall and conical against the sky near a thin stream the whites called Sand Creek. There they would spend the cold of winter under the protection of the United States Cavalry commanded by Major Edward Wynkoop, a friend.

Lines

wolf
   tracks
   deep in snow
never to travel
behind another travois

bright feather
   on the path
   cut deep
   into earth
   or on mountain crust

spirit
echo

   voices
on a long journey
   in prairie winds

Sand Creek

Ponoeohe (Sand Creek), the little dried river, had been a favorite campground for as many winters as old men could count. Since first separating from their northern brothers, who possessed the Sacred Buffalo Hat and lived near the sacred *PaSapa*, the Black Hills, the *Hewa-ta-niuw* Cheyenne had enjoyed life along the green banks of the *Ponoeohe*.

When the moon of the falling leaves
rose to greet the dark hand of night,
it rose above lodges of the southern people, its warm
light
protected their sleep
and held their bundle of Sacred Arrows
in trust and safety.

Ponoeohe, called Sand Creek by the *vehos*,
loaned the people its clear waters to drink,
its grass for their ponies to eat

and cottonwoods and willows that grew ever so thinly
along the banks
gave to the *Tsististas*
winter protection
and gave sapling twigs
for both the sweat lodge and for arrows,
and the cottonwood gave its bark in the long cold winter
to the pony herds for forage.

Rabbits, turtles, and coyotes lived near the stream
and when needed could be taken for whatever purpose,
food or clothing, ornament

or story.

The *Ponoeohe* raced swiftly in spring across the plains and had in ancient times cut high bluffs into the level land that afforded the people refuge and respite from the blusterous winds that swept across the earth from faraway *Wah-to-Yah*, the Spanish Peaks.

These bluffs could be used for scouting and sending signals; and here roots and berries could be found, and the birds that flew in to eat the ripe berries could be caught for decorative feathers. Sometimes a bear would wander down from the mountains and could be hunted for food, a deliciously different taste from the strict diet of buffalo meat.

For millennia, the buffalo thundered by *Ponoeohe* as thick as the grains of dust in the storm that often whirled across the flatlands in the moon of the summer hunt.

Maheo was thanked profoundly for these fine gifts.

Maheo, the Great Power (*Heammawihio*), had given the *Wi-ta-pi-u* a good way of life. The Great Power gave them *Ponoeohe*, gave them the earth and the winds that brought the rain, gave them the *pte* and the swiftness of the arrow.

Maheo gave them breath in the morning and sleep at night.

Maheo gave the *Wi-ta-pi-u* food, mothers for their children and strong warriors, and wise elders to advise and lead the *Tsististas*.

On returning from a trip north for the Sun Dance with their brothers of the Sacred Buffalo Hat, a child wandering around looking for buffalo chips to make a fire discovered two trails cutting across the smooth valley and winding over the bluffs of *Ponoeohe*. He called to the people. The women pitched their tipis but all waited to see what creature would return again to cut deeper the ruts of these parallel trails.

Many sleeps came but during the month of thin snows a strange travois on rolling stones rumbled down the trail. The vehicle stopped and *vehos* offered coffee and sugar to the headmen of the band.

In signs they made it known that their wagons were rolling towards a *veho* village called Bent's Fort on the Arkansas River and then would roll on to the Spanish country and its trade-village, Santa Fe.

The people greeted the whites with cordiality and respect, feasted them on buffalo and dog and accepted with gratitude presents of coffee, blankets, an iron kettle and a few trinkets. For these they exchanged buffalo fur, and when the whites saw how beautifully the furs had been preserved they encouraged a few headchiefs to travel with them to the Arkansas, to Bent's Fort, to trade further for more goods.

When the chiefs returned they told the people about the wooden village and of a black-white woman, Charolette Green, who cooked there over fires of cottonwood and willow
                              —and of the fire water of the whites that made you have grand visions and left you sick and empty the next morning.

Ponoeohe swelled in spring and overflowed, yet dried to not much more than a thin trickle in summer. The people came, were happy at its banks, and left for the north to the Platte, or traveled south to the Washita near the Antelope Hills, but *Ponoeohe* remained their favorite camping grounds.

Each time on returning to the little dried creek they were to discover more *vehos*, and that the wagons' wheels had cut deeper into their free and open lands. One year they found nearly all the cottonwoods cut down for firewood, piles of cold ashes along the craggy bluffs of *Ponoeohe*.

Rabbits and turtles were seldom seen in the grasses, and buffalo trailed further and further away from Sand Creek.

As word of the gold in Colorado spread, more whites arrived. But instead of passing into the mountains, as they had during the California Gold Rush of 1849, they built towns and settled down to stay. The Indians, who had no need for gold, continued to accept the emigrants, but as more and more arrived, the buffalo on which the tribes depended for their very survival were frightened off or killed.

Denver City continued to grow, and "troubles" festered as the Indians, dispossessed, hungry, and angry, became restless and contemptuous of all the encroachment.

In April of 1860, a group of white men visited an Arapaho camp near their town. When the men were gone, they raped some of the women and stole some of the mules.

Reprisals were threatened by Chief Left Hand.

Commissioner of Indian Affairs, A. B. Greenwood, recognized that the only alternative to peaceful coexistence with the Indians was to exterminate them. This was not, he believed, an acceptable alternative, and he recommended that a new treaty be worked out.

The Cheyenne and Arapaho people were invited to Fort Wise to sign this treaty in February of 1861. Under the agreement, the Indians would relinquish their claims to all lands except a gameless, arid section of southeastern Colorado Territory, which was to serve as a reservation for them.

In return, the United States agreed to protect the Indians on the reservation, to pay them the sum of $30,000 a year for fifteen years, and to provide them with the stock, tools, and buildings necessary for them to farm their lands. John Smith, who had reappeared with a new Indian wife, served as translator during the Fort Wise treaty meetings, and a postscript to the treaty awarded half-bloods Robert Bent and Jack Smith each 640 acres of choice land along the Arkansas Valley.

When the American Civil War began that same spring, Union troops were recalled east to fight the Confederacy. Those troops left in the west were thin in number, poorly equipped, and suffered from low morale. The summer of 1861 was hot and dry and the country became parched.

The tribes, who had not received the provisions promised by the treaty, were hungry. Several thousand gathered around the fort, threatening its security. They were temporarily quieted by the dispersal of a few provisions, but the Treaty of Fort Wise was never honored.

In May the Cheyenne and Arapaho tribes held a secret meeting with the Sioux north of Denver for the purpose of uniting and driving the white settlers from the country. The Indians made it known that they considered the treaty of Fort Wise a swindle. Black Kettle and White Antelope both denied signing it, and the Cheyenne refused to leave their hunting grounds and go to the assigned reservation where there was no game or means for survival.

Skirmishes continued throughout 1863.

Wagon trains were attacked and the roads closed to traffic. Denver was blocked. The Union not only needed the gold from Colorado's mines but it also feared an alliance between the Confederacy and the Indians.

In 1864, the Hungate family, who had been peaceful farmers, were brutally murdered. Their mutilated bodies were brought to Denver and displayed to the people, touching off panic, anger, and talk of revenge.

This atrocity was blamed on Roman Nose, a Cheyenne and member of the Dog Soldiers, the main warrior contingent.

In June, John Evans, governor of the Colorado Territory, issued a proclamation directing all friendly Indians to go to places of safety, where they were to be given provisions. The object of this, he said, was to prevent friendly Indians from being killed through mistake.

The Cheyenne and Arapaho from the Arkansas Valley area were directed to report to Fort Lyon.

Black Kettle accepted this offer, and his people set up their camp about forty miles away on Sand Creek, where they were soon joined by other bands, two-thirds of which were women and children. The post commander, Major John Anthony, assured Black Kettle that they would all be safe there and told them to go out and hunt buffalo until such time as provisions could be acquired for them.

Monahsetah was seventeen when the bluecoats attacked her people at *Ponoeohe*, Sand Creek.

In the old days winter was a gentle, sleepy time: old men
would gather before the fires of the lodges and tell
great tales of the past and spin stories
of the Cheyenne ancient life in the north.
Light and dark
grazed across the plains like antelope. Women sat in shadows
of the lodge chewing pieces of hide for moccasins.

Young braves prepared shields and arrowheads
for the war games
of spring and summer when the ponies were fat
on new grass.

Tending fires, grandmothers would sing songs
as a hunter worked the soft
fur of a freshly killed rabbit or beaver,
or an old man would blow
upon a cedar flute decorated with carved snake heads
with bright feathers and hide-strings of beads
flowing from the mouth. Young men wove music
to attract the young women of the village.

The old days were quiet, days of peace and plenty.

There were always twigs and buffalo chips to gather for the fires, bark to
strip from cottonwoods to feed shaggy ponies, and occasionally a hunting
party would be sent out for fresh game. Sometimes a young Brave
returned with pelts of coyote which he prepared for sacred ceremonies.

Work consisted of keeping fires, cooking meals when there was food,
making clothing and moccasins, or working beaded goods.

Time for games,
time for singing,
time for prayers of thanks to the Great Spirit.

Time for feasting and gambling.

It was very cold. Much time was spent in love
between buffalo furs.

But this winter the people were hungry and there was short time for stories and flutes. Women spent days in the low hills of the flats pushing snow off accumulated mounds to dig out a few roots not frozen.

Boys were sent out to beat brush for rabbits and chipmunks, and hunters were far away from the village for many sleeps scouting the plains for deer or stray buffalo, or raiding the *veho* ranches for food.

Monahsetah was sent with the girls and women to pull roots and collect chips. Though her father was a second chief she was allowed no greater portion of food than any other villager, and was given an equal share of the work. She would return to her lodge hungry and cold, her back aching and her feet and fingers nearly frozen.

Each day teetered between survival of the Cheyenne and death.

Father, I come;
Mother, I come;
Brother, I come;
Father, give us the arrows.

Chankpe Opi Wakpala!

Father, I hold one for Big Foot;
Mother, I hold one for Black Coyote;
Brother, I hold one for Yellow Bird;
Father, give us back the arrows.

Chankpe Opi Wakpala!

Father, give us sky;
Father, give us sun in the east;
Father, give us night in the west;
Father, watch our shadows;
Father, give us back our arrows.

Chankpe Opi Wakpala!

Mother, your breast is bare;
Mother, your breast was not enough to sustain us;
Mother, hold our bones now;
Mother, we search for our arrows.

The Sand Creek Massacre
November 29, 1864

A sharp, clear, cold night enclosed the land. Bright stars canopied the plains.

A wolf howled and its pups yipped in answer at the moving shadows of trees weaving at the banks of the freezing stream. In the night the newly formed teeth of the ice commenced to chew at the shoreline. Small fires glittered along the edge of the pony herds. Young boys sent to guard the animals warmed tingling fingers and toes at the flames.

In War Bonnet's lodge, pitched far upstream, sat the trader John Smith and his son, Jack. William Bent's two sons, George and the adolescent, Charley, were in the lodge as well. One Eye spoke with Smith and the others.

Slightly downstream, on the north bank but wedged off from the creek, White Antelope's old wife had pitched her lodge. The fire within glowed only a pale light. Nearby stood the painted lodge of Yellow Wolf . . . which was dark.

Further downstream, and well within the great bend of the creek, rose the black conical tipi of Black Kettle. A high fire danced within the wrinkled shadows against the hide wall. The movement of the occupants, though stilted, writhed in the bright light.

Not so far off, Edmund Guerrier, half-breed son of Bill Guerrier, slept in the arms of his young wife, Julia, Monahsetah's friend and William Bent's youngest offspring.

Monahsetah, seventeen, only slightly younger than Julia, slept soundly in her father's lodge safe from wolf and warm from cold night air. Temperatures dropped drastically. Night snapped colder. Pools of the creek froze and cracked. Hungry wolves barked; village dogs scavenged the streets for bones tossed away by the women.

The fires of the herders sputtered out. Only a frail spiral of smoke rose to the nest of stars above. The boys slept.

The lateness of the hour settled upon the village.

Tipis stood in quiet darkness like ghostly pyramids of stone or snow. Not a dog barked or growled in greed over a dry bone; not a horse neighed, nor baby whispered. The camp's central fire crinkled peacefully, innocently. An old man threw in buffalo chips and twigs occasionally to maintain light.

The oppressive cold hung hard and heavy against the night.

Only the snap of a cottonwood branch disturbed the village.

Hesitantly the first glint of light shot a lance across the far horizon. Light hovered at the thin border, then rose slowly and spread as it climbed morning sky. Day broke.

Women awoke and trudged to the creek to fetch water. As they cracked the icy pools in which to drop their pots or skins, they heard in the distance the loud rumble of hoofs thudding against the earth.

They gave out a cry to awaken the men—there were only a handful of men in the camp. Major Scott J. Anthony, the new commander of Fort Lyon who had replaced the Tall Chief Wynkoop recently, had sent the warrior-hunters off to find game, saying that he could no longer dole out provisions.

The women cried out that buffalo approached. The men slept on.

At last the raucous yapping of the dogs began to shake the village to wakefulness. The Smiths, father and son, in War Bonnet's lodge, with the two soldiers, awoke.

Old Yellow Wolf prepared to bathe at the creek.

White Antelope lay still in his warm robes.

Day broke.

The cottonwoods at the creek edge stood bare and tall, white with frost. On the south bank of Sand Creek, the ponies stomped for warmth and their steaming breaths rose into the daylight. Not yet dawn, the young herders slept.

Again the women at the creek called out that animals approached. As the dark spot on the plains grew larger the women recognized the vast blur to be not buffalo but a command of soldiers.

One of the women ran to War Bonnet's lodge. She knew "Uncle" John Smith was there. She called for him to come out. Another woman ran to Black Kettle. Rushing within his lodge, she cried out that bluecoats were on the plains riding into the village from the south in two long lines.

Black Kettle sprang up and went out into the brittle morning. He raised the American flag that A.B. Greenwood, the Commissioner of Indian Affairs, had given him in 1860 at the Fort Wise Treaty along with a white flag of peace at the 1860 signing of the Fort Wise Treaty.

He was confident that the American flag would protect his village.

The quiet, sleepy village churned into a beehive with people rushing about, noisy in fear and anxiety.

> Brother, we cried for you;
> Brother, we called you back;
> Brother, we descended with you.
> and your flesh
> > and your bones
> > and your fur which kept us warm;
> Brother, when our arrows are returned
> > we will seek you.

Chankpe Opi Wakpala!

> Arrows, now the skies are diseased;
> Arrows, now the earth is diseased;
> Arrows, now the people are sick on dreams;
> Arrows, come back to us.

Chankpe Opi Wakpala!

Troops loomed on the southern horizon. Their guns and sabers glistened in the rising light of morning.

Little Rock awakened his family at the shouting. He called to his wife and shook Monahsetah and the younger children. The girl rose, dressed quickly, and throwing a blanket around her shoulders, ran from the lodge into the streets at her father's heels as he had directed.

The army command, stretching like two bare branches of a cottonwood, streaming out like rolling ribbons, reached the bluffs over the creek to the right of the camp.

Here the force split.

One battalion bore straight onward and crossed the stream to circle the north flanks of the village. The third division crawled more slowly and advanced from the right flank with howitzers, directly left upstream and took a route through the ice-covered pools of the creek bed.

The village, like an anthill that had been stepped upon, splintered at the first rifle shot.

Cries and yells tore open the village streets.

An attack!

The people, disorganized and bewildered, raced to Black Kettle for protection. He was found standing beneath his flags with his wife, Woman Here-After (*Ar-no-ho-won*) and White Antelope.

Rifle fire was heard coming from the herds corralled below the creek southeast of War Bonnet's lodge. A group of young Braves rushed to the ponies. Black Kettle called his terrified people about him. Baffled, they huddled in thin clothing, teeth chattering from the cold.

In the excitement many had left not fully dressed. Women stood with only a blanket wrapped about their bare shoulders. Men shivered with little more on than breechclouts. Children crept in under the blankets and nestled against mothers' thighs.

Black Kettle attempted to calm the gathered people.

The chief told them that there must be a mistake, and not to be afraid.

They were at peace with the soldiers, and their chiefs in Denver and at Fort Lyon had sent the Cheyenne to Sand Creek. They were not only peaceful Indians but were there on the creek under the protection of the cavalry.

There must be a mistake.

Our father is gone;
Our father has fled;
Our father has turned his face;
Arrows, give us back our father.

Our mother has closed her eyes;
Our mother has closed her mouth;
Our mother has closed her heart;
Arrows, give us back our mother.

Our brother has wandered away;
Our brother does not walk;
Our brother has gone down;
Arrows, give us back our brother.

Monahsetah pushed and elbowed her way through the milling group. She stared at her uncle, the old sachem. What help, what protection could he or his flags offer. She, freezing in the morning cold, drew her blanket together.

Again the chief spoke not to be frightened.

The troops opened fire on the huddled mass of women, children and old who instantly fractured into a run. The crack of rifles dispersed the Cheyenne and, in struggling parties, they made a dash upstream away from the advancing army that galloped screaming and yowling into the village. Black Kettle, his wife, and White Antelope stood fast by the lodge under the protective flags of truce and peace fluttering in the wind.

Monahsetah halted in her race. Chief Spotted Crow fell.

She screamed and rushed after the others who fled the headmen's lodge. At nearly every turn now the crack of rifles felled a Cheyenne. The howling people zigzagged to escape the line of fire but older ones fell. Frozen with fear Monahsetah wandered half-blind with anxiety and horror in search of her mother and father. She made her way, stumbling upstream in the push of the others.

The three separate battalions of soldiers advanced into and around the village.

The young men, the Braves who had rushed off to save the pony herds were met with fire and were able to rope only a few horses and mules. Mounted, they escaped the attacked village and rode toward Smoky Hill where the Dog Soldiers under Tall Bull and the people under the leadership of Stone Forehead and Little Raven were villaged seventy miles to the north.

At the first gunfire, John Smith threw down his breakfast, and, with a white handkerchief tied to a cottonwood stick, advanced toward the troops. Confident that he would not be taken for an Indian, he walked into the fray. Before he had gone 200 yards, the troops fired upon him. One soldier rose in his saddle and yelled out, "Shoot the son of a bitch, he is no better than an Indian."

Smith, with Louderback, one of the soldiers who had spent the night in War Bonnet's lodge, sped back into the depths of the village.

Ed Gurrier, with his young wife, Julia Bent, and Jack Smith escaped the village. Smith was captured later by Major Hal Sayr and returned to the bombarded camp.

Among the first to fall in the massacre were Left Hand, War Bonnet, Two Thighs, and One Eye (Major Anthony's spy).

The aging chief and his wife maintained positions by the lodge beneath the fluttering flags riddled with bullets. They remained long after the others had fled upstream. Small parties fled west where there were banks of loose sand in which they could dig defensive pits. Black Kettle realized finally the futility of staying in the emptied besieged village.

He had no power nor weapon to stem the attack. His flags were useless in the faces of the very same people who had given them to him.
The symbol was an empty one.

His people and what few warriors remained in the camp were running off for their lives. Those left were dead.

The ancient Yellow Wolf, almost eighty years old, had been dropped near the stream.

Bear Man, Porcupine Bear had been killed.

Yellow Shield sprawled dead on the earth in a puddle of his blood.

The arrows broke at Greasy Grass;
The arrows broke with Crazy Horse;
The arrows broke with Sitting Bull;
Father, give us back our arrows.

Chankpe Opi Wakpala!

In the river of his blood,
       I stand in Bigfoot's grave;
In the shout of fear,
       I shout for Black Coyote;
In the dance of his dream,
       I dance for Yellow Bird;
Father, give us back our arrows.

We will put the center back
      in your country;
We will circle stones and make the hoop
      in your country;
We will plant the seed of the sacred tree
      in your country.

Black Kettle with Woman Hereafter urged White Antelope to flee to safe grounds. Adamant in his plan and plea for peace, the old chief, nearing seventy-five years, walked nobly into the cold stream.

White Antelope stood with arms folded in the symbol of peace, and sang his death song:

> *Nothing lives long*
> *Except the earth and the mountain . . .*

Arms crossing his chest, each hand to a shoulder blade White Antelope stood singing.

A shock of surprise contorted his face.

His eyes tightened in disbelief. He could feel something hot spill down his flesh as his deerskin shirt darkened with moisture. His head bent, his legs buckled. He slumped and fell into the freezing waters of *Ponoeohe*, Sand Creek.

White Antelope's body was found so mutilated it was barely recognizable. His ears and fingers had been chopped off for their rings. His privates had been cut off. A soldier had made his scrotum into a tobacco pouch.

The old man who had trekked to Denver to seek peace with the whites had found it at last in the grave . . . or rather, in death. His corpse never received a proper burial but was left on the cold tundra of the plains to the appetites of wolves. The last shred of dignity was denied this peaceful man.

But better to feed wolves
        than be manure
                for the whiteman's
                        vegetable garden.

The wolf had never done him harm.
			He was his brother.
And the wolf, too, would go in the poisons of the ranchers,
the sport of a new breed of hunters, a breed that knew no satiety,
no bounds, no rules, no ethics,
no compassion for the two-legged or the four-legged,
the winged or those of the water,

no compassion for the water itself,

nor the earth, mother earth whose body the water flowed across
and slaked the thirst of all the Great Spirit's creatures,
nor even Father Sun.

Wind, not wolves, would now howl
across these empty plains, howl and scatter the echoes
of the old voices, the ancient ones,
and the voices of those that were to die that dawn.

Wolf, eat while you still may, even this flesh
of ones who loved and understood you,
for your mourning, too, was coming;
prepare your death song, hopefully your women will survive
to sing your death, wail your passing. No woman now
wailed for White Antelope, chief to the Cheyenne,
son of the bright morning and the long night,
father of the day.

His blood brightened the ice upon the creek bed.

Black Kettle and Woman Hereafter struggled to the sand pits where a large party of Cheyenne held off the troops. They fought fiercely with few weapons and little ammunition.

Women fought at the side of the men. On the way to the sand pits, Woman Here-after was shot. Her riddled body collapsed as if a tipi with the poles pulled down, or a blanket that fluttered with wind and then became suddenly windless.

The chief said a fast prayer over his wife's bloodied body, and left her for dead. He sped on into the straggling parties of his people running pell-mell across the open prairie. After the first attack subsided, the aging chief returned to the stream for his wife's corpse, and he found she had been shot ten times but still lived. He managed to hoist her to a horse and took her north to safety.

John Smith, once more, attempted to reach the white troops. He called out to the commander, Colonel John Milton Chivington, as he marched astride his white steed up the creek bed. Chivington, thirsty for Indian blood, shouted to his men "Remember the Platte," and "Take no prisoners . . . and don't forget nits make lice," inciting the men to vile atrocities against the children as well, the nits who would grow up to be "lice."

Chivington caught hold of "Uncle" John in the melee and called for the soldiers who had spent the night in War Bonnet's lodge, and for Charley Bent, William's youngest son. Smith clung to the stirrups of a soldier and walked along upstream where he discovered Cheyenne entrenched in the rifle pits. Nearly two hundred soldiers had the Indians surrounded and picked them off, women and men, like tin cans on a fence post.

In a short time the soldiers had routed and killed most of the Indians.

Monahsetah fled Black Kettle's lodge and hurried on upstream where lay the hacked corpse of Chief Standing Water.

She watched a soldier approach a woman lying on the banks of the stream. The woman's leg had been shattered by a howitzer shell. When she raised her arm to plead for her life, the soldier struck the fallen woman with his saber. He broke her arm. Screaming in excruciating pain, she rolled over and raised a second arm in protection, and again the soldier struck her with his saber.

Screaming, the woman buried her face in the earth to await the death blow. The soldier went off and left her struggling between life and death.

The soldier turned in the direction of a girl who had been crouching near. She raised up and threw open her blanket to prove she was a woman. It was believed that whites did not harm or kill women. The soldier drove his sword through her groin.

Monahsetah ran west. She felt a bullet shatter her left leg, just below the knee. She heard her own voice cry out, one sharp cry. Then she mastered her voice, breathing through her teeth.

She lay still for three sharp breaths before pressing into action.

She kicked with her right leg, crawling and scraping forward, dragging her shattered leg behind her, until she rolled forward into the sand pits. She pulled a cottonwood branch and fallen leaves over her legs, smeared the blood from her wound onto her cheeks and forehead and lay still as if dead.

Women ran out from the sheltering banks of the creek and the sand pits and exposed their persons. While begging for life and mercy they were shot down and ripped open with bayonets.

One woman lying on the earth had been cut open and an unborn child lay at her side.

The dead—scalped, hacked and split open—were found for five miles along the stream from the village. Babies had been smashed by rifle butts; women had their dresses torn open and their privates slashed; men had their privates severed, and, in certain cases, stuffed in their mouths.

Practically all were scalped, even children and infants—trophies and proof of victory.

Seventy-five bodies were counted by Smith; a few aging warriors but more women and children. Most were scalped and some mutilated, body parts taken back to the parade that awaited them in Denver: scalps, scrotums and breasts would hang like banners to parade the streets of Denver for the cheering crowds.

We will fill the river with water;
We will fill the woods with trees;
We will clothe the bones with flesh;
We will empty the graves;
We will call back the wolf, the deer;
We will build the walls of the dream;
We will make and tend the fire,
            in your country.

For I am the Sun!

I am the sun!

I stand above the world.

Chankpe Opi Wakpala!
Chankpe Opi Wakpala!

Little Bear, later, told George Bent that after the fight he saw soldiers scalping the dead and saw an old woman who had been scalped by the soldiers trying to walk about, but unable to see where to go. Her whole scalp had been taken and the skin of the forehead fell down over her eyes.

George Bent related to George Bird Grinnell:

> *The soldiers concentrated their fire on the people in the pits, and we fought back as well as we could with guns and bows, but we only had a few guns. The troops did not rush in and fight hand to hand, but once or twice after they had killed many of the men in a certain pit, they rushed in and finished up the work, killing the wounded and the women and children that had not been hurt. The fight here was kept up until nearly sundown, when at last the commanding officer (Chivington) called off his men and all started back down the creek toward the camp that they had expelled us from. As they went back, the soldiers scalped the dead lying in the bed of the stream and cut up the bodies in a manner no Indian could equal.*

> *My brother Charlie was in the camp, and he and Jack Smith, another half-blood, were captured. After the fight the soldiers took Jack Smith out and shot him in cold blood . . . fortunately among the troops were a number of New Mexican scouts whom Charlie knew, and these young fellows protected him.*

Soon after the troops left us, we came out of the pits and begun to move slowly up the stream. More than half of us were wounded and all were on foot . . . I was so badly wounded that I could hardly walk.

When our party had gone about ten miles above the captured camp, we went into a ravine and stopped there for the night. It was very dark and bitterly cold. Very few of us had warm clothing for we had been driven out of our beds and had no time to dress. The wounded suffered greatly. There was no wood to be had, but the unwounded men and women collected grass and made fires. The wounded men were placed near the fire and covered with grass to keep them from freezing. All night long the people kept up a constant hallooing to attract the attention of any Indians who might be wandering about in the sand hills. We left the comfortless ravine before day and started east toward a Cheyenne camp on the Smoky Hill, forty or fifty miles away . . . We were obliged to look out for a large number of women and children. In fact, it was on the women and children that the brunt of this terrible business fell. Over three-fourths of the people killed in the battle were women and children.

A year after this attack on our camp a number of investigations of the occurrence were made. Colonel Chivington's friends were then extremely anxious to prove our camp was hostile, but they had no facts in support of their statements.

One of Chivington's most trusted officers said:

When we came upon this camp on Sand Creek we did not care whether these particular Indians were friendly or not. It was well known to everybody in Denver that the Colonel's orders to his troops were to kill Indians, to 'kill all, little or big.'

Father give us back our arrows,
        and make a woman into a child,
        a boy into a man,
        a girl into a woman,
        an arrow into a country,
        a country into a home,
        a home into the sun.

Chankpe Opi Wakpala!
Chankpe Opi Wakpala!
Chankpe Opi Wakpala!

Father, give us no more graves;
Father, give us back our arrows!
We have learned to hold them sacred!

Chivington's dawn massacre of the peaceful Cheyenne opened a new war which flamed for nearly twenty years across the southern plains. The agonized cries of the wounded Cheyenne trailed the winds north to the warring Lakota (Sioux) who joined with their brothers to fight the white man and to hold off their own extermination.

Shortly after the massacre, George Bent and his brother, Charlie, whose mother, Owl Woman, died while birthing him, ran off to the village of the Dog Soldiers. For some three years these two brothers raised the lance of fired revenge and lowered the bullets of death into innocent whites, whites who did not participate in the Sand Creek Massacre and had no knowledge of the atrocity.

Black Kettle trailed north with the remnants of his band, and for a time raised the war club. He joined forces with their warring Cheyenne and the Dog Soldiers. White scalps dangled again from the lodge poles of his village, and victory was danced about the fires raging against the darkness of the night. The aging sachem was once more recognized, for a short duration, as headman of all Arkansas Cheyenne. His word was law.

Once the chief's anger and hunger for revenge subsided, he came to realize the futility of waging war upon the white man.

Whites were like sands of the desert, blown about by the winds of fate and fortune. It would take an eternity to carry those grains away; it would take the Indian into total extinction to attempt stemming the flow of those pale faces.

A wise and noble chief, Black Kettle had fought long and hard against the Pawnee and Ute as a young man, and later against the white soldiers.

He had lost the bundle of Sacred Arrows to the Pawnee and his first wife, White Buffalo Woman, forty years before to the Ute. He lost his land and life to the whites. Surely he came to realize and accept through vision, instinct and intelligence, that the struggle with the whites was as futile as the evasion of death.

It ceased to be important to fight whites, to lose young men in battle in order to celebrate an unenduring victory and peace; it was useless to roll the tail of his pony and ride off to halt the iron-horse or the conestoga wagons, to drive them from off his mother earth.

The Europeans were on the plains to stay; their sod huts put down roots into the soil and they not only grew leaves but children whose roots crept even deeper into the earth.

White Antelope's prayer for peace and Yellow Wolf's hope of farming still held firmly in Black Kettle's heart. Certainly the enemy could be reasoned with, a compromise made between them. There was land for all. War was a waste of good Indian flesh and blood and doomed his people to extermination or hungry wards of the government.

He would join the whites in brotherhood and save what peoples, what customs, were left to safeguard.

He trailed south with Little Rock and his daughter, Monahsetah. On October 12, 1865, at the Treaty of the Little Arkansas, the old chief made, in part, this speech:

> *The Great Father above hears us, and the Great Father at Washington will hear what we have to say. It is true that you came here from Washington, and it is true what you say here today. The Big Chief, he gave his words to me to come and meet you here, and I take hold and retain what he says. I believe it all to be true, and think it is all true. Their young white men, when I meet them on the plains, I give them my horse and my moccasins, and I am glad today to think that the Great Father has sent good men to take pity on us.*
>
> *We are living friendly now.*

The chief begged General Sanborn, president of the peace commission, to open the north road that his people still in the Platte country might travel south unharmed. At the head of the caravan, he led his tattered band into the unknown lands south of the Arkansas River in Comanche-Kiowa territory along the Cimarron River between the Canadian and Red Rivers.

He led them into Custer's jaw.

Chivington and his fellow butchers, even after the investigations into the wanton slaughter at Sand Creek, had truly won the battle. Black Kettle and his band were finally exiled from Colorado into the wastes of Indian Territory, Oklahoma. Not only the gold of the Rockies fell into the bank vaults of Denver and eventually the industrial east, but the grazing lands of the plains were opened wide to ranching and the cattlemen. The iron-horse sped a new economy into the west. Colorado entered the Union of States and its Native "savage pests" were rid of cheaply and permanently denied life and subsistence in the lands roamed by the shadows of their ancestors.

Roman Nose

Cheyenne Warrior Killed at the Battle
of Arikaree Fork, September 17, 1868

Warrior, where your pony pranced on your mother's breast
Grey cities rise to break the sky;
Cheyenne, where your father sang in the Almighty's sun
Rivers flood and cottonwoods wither.

Ripe plums hang in the afternoon.
The Father waited;
Dark plums hung in the twilight,
The Father waited.
Blood fell from the tree of his body
While the Father waited.
In the blue dusk at the river's edge
He sighed and rolled his eyes:
The Father looked down
And sucked his breath.

      Women cried and slashed their wrists;
      Women cried and cut their hair;
      His pony was led to slaughter;
      Women cried and slashed their legs.

Grass grew between his teeth,
Grass grew through his fingers;
Streams flowed from his lips;
Deer came from his breast;
A wolf howled upon his cheek;
A bear hunched on his eyelids;
Grass grew between his teeth, and birds came;
Bats, hawks, kingfishers;
Eagles flew down to his scaffold, and crows;
Youth blew into flutes.
Grass grew through his fingers.

Drums stilled,
Rattles shook,
Dancers
Pantomimed in fire light.

They covered his flesh with ripe plums;
They covered his flesh with hide;
Wolf came, the deer;
Buffalo came, bat came;
His arms were two arrows;
His legs were two lances;
From the dust of his loins
Rose a cottonwood and it flowers the plains.

Father, take his horse;
Father, take his arrows;
Father, take his feathers;
Father, take his anger.

Over the grass that grew between his teeth
A nation marched;
Over the grass that grew between his fingers
Buffalo passed, elk, wild peas passed
Into the dusk of his groin;
The ancient lands once covered with grass
Blazed fire,
Charred under the sun,
Under swords,
Under cattle and wheat.

Winds swept off the mountains
Blew his feather, his breath;
Blew the dust of his mother . . .
Nothing lasts long but rocks . . .

Warrior, the iron has rusted upon the earth;
Cheyenne, the useless grass is trampled;
Cattle diseased, the sheep hungry;
Warrior, gold has been split from the mountains!

The scars of your children shine and burst in the East;
The morning door of the lodge is closed;
Warrior, a boy climbs the knoll to dream;
Cheyenne, the fire waits to be lighted
In the ashes of the grey cities, the wheat.
You did not die for nothing . . .
It was a good day to die
Under the plums, the eagle's flight.

Black Kettle left behind in the cottonwood graveyard of the earth the spirits of the old ones. Never again would he hear the voice of Lean Bear, or Yellow Wolf, Tobacco, or his elder brother, White Antelope on the tongue of the winds. In his removal, they had been at last silenced.

William Bent, broken and aging himself, remained the old chief's friend to the last. The free life both had known and enjoyed as young men, brothers, was finished. The plains were soon to be fenced like their lives. Bent's last years were spent aiding Black Kettle as his interpreter and closest advisor, proof of the strong ties of men who did not share blood but shared the quality of humanity.

The Sand Creek Massacre led to a holocaust. Chivington lit a fire that burned across the western plains for nearly two decades. The results were not only the decimation of the Plains Indians but heavy suffering for the white population as well.

To this day *Ponoeohe*, Sand Creek, flows through Chivington Ranch.

Sand Creek Colorado
100 years after

night thick as heavy voices
or the plod of cattle rattling
in the farmer's garbage dump

coyotes called ancient shadows
Cheyenne whose fires burn low along the creek
to light the collection of the dead
bones wolves chose not to chew

the state marker says nothing
of the women, the children
or White Antelope's cry . . .
"nothing lasts but grass and mountains . . ."
choked by the butt of his penis
soldier's thought a joke

wandering in sacred screams
holy terror and extermination
picking the snot of gold from Chivington's nose
he stuffed to the stench of his kill

thin hands found our faces
our dog whined and hid beneath the Datsun
hungry mouths of children
sought her breasts and would have sucked
had she opened her blouse

sleep was safe in New York
exhausted in the numb and nulled morning
we counted cigarette packages, beer cans
orange peels and civilization
and left the dead to comfort the dying

while in the dark birds sing

history's blood has grown its spring crop of grass
tall cottonwoods stand central to the scholar
lofty rock peak dawn to citron morning

1866

Little Eagle, a respected warrior ten years older than Monahsetah, had been courting her off and on for the past three years. She had some affection for him but remained proud and superior, refusing to marry him no matter how much game he brought to the family, no matter how many gifts of jewelry carved from deer antler or songs played on his cedar flute.

Little Eagle had other options, but he was madly in love with the proud and intelligent chief's daughter, Monahsetah.

He had one last plan. He departed from the band for several days, and no one knew where he had gone. When he returned he had eleven beautiful horses, a "necklace of horses" he called them, all those colors tied together. A beautiful sight. He presented the horses to her father, Little Rock, who was, himself, rather exasperated by his daughter's refusal to choose a husband. Monahsetah's mother, Skunk Woman, also supported the wedding, as she was concerned that Monahsetah would become pregnant before a ceremony bound her daughter to a man in the eyes of the Cheyenne Nation and Maheo.

Little Rock agreed, and the two were married soon after. It was Monahsetah's turn to pass through the sacred rites.

For the first few months, Little Eagle slept apart from Monahsetah, giving her proper respect until she truly "chose" him. They slept in the same tipi but separated, symbolically, by a quiver of arrows. To him the arrows symbolized the future children they would have together and his commitment to protect her. To her the arrows symbolized all the pain that would come to him if he crossed the line.

She did not dislike Little Eagle, and she recognized his adoration of her, but she often refused to do women's work for him and his family. She retorted that he was lucky to have her, that the daughter of a chief deserved better than him and his eleven horses. She was bitter that her fate could be decided by horses.

Little Eagle became increasingly bitter over time, impatient and lonely by her pride and refusal.

And his friends and brothers never stopped teasing him, bragging about the hours of love they spent each night in their tipis, asking if he was "cold last night," then lifting up their children to shame him.

Little Eagle was determined to woo Monahsetah with a combination of kindness and strength. He was a strong man but did not have a honey tongue. He showed his love through gifts, through the notes on his flute, through the objects of beauty and usefulness he made for her or acquired through trade. He showed his love through patience.

He showed his love by doing the work that would normally be done by the women. But as the daughter of a chief, Monahsetah saw this as weakness. Still, Little Eagle believed that in time her heart would accept him. If only she understood how strongly he loved her.

At last, Little Eagle could wait no longer. He came to her in the night and forced her legs apart.

In the months that followed, there was a combination of love and violence between them. At times, she moaned under his love or atop his powerful body. At times she even sought him out by hanging up the quiver of arrows and waiting for him on his side of the tipi, but after their love-making, she would always roll away from him and sleep alone once more.

She never stopped comparing him, unfavorably, to her noble father, Chief Little Rock.

Little Eagle's jealousy and control only grew stronger, until her contempt for him grew more powerful than her love.

She refused him again and again, until he once again tried to force her legs apart, pinning her down and kissing her face so hard it hurt. She managed to free one arm and reach for the small gun she had hidden nearby. She tried to shoot off his penis in a moment of inspiration, but instead struck him in the knee.

He howled so loudly the whole camp awakened and there were voices outside the tent. She didn't wait for him to hit her, but fled the tipi and escaped to her father, Little Rock, for protection. Her father agreed that it was only safe for her to remain with him and to consider the marriage annulled. He returned the eleven horses to Little Eagle.

By now, however, a child was growing inside of her. In a few months, she named the newborn baby, Bird Girl, for her crying sounded more like singing and she had a weak appetite.

Soon after, in November of 1868, the Cheyenne were attacked on the Washita. Monahsetah was barely 20 years old.

2000

The history of a people is not merely the story of its wars, conquests, blood spilled and death, nor is the rise or fall of a civilization measured this way. A civilization is inextricably comprised of its arts, of its rituals, inventions, of its oral literature and collective memory, of song and poetry as markers of the people's spiritual accomplishments. A civilization is comprised of individual moments of friendship, laughter, problem solving, the daily intimacy of the family space, between parents and children and between lovers, all the moments of public and private triumph and despair.

The clay pot's replacement by the iron pot is one factor that undermined Native civilization, with far-reaching consequences. The women found the iron pot significantly easier to cook in and transport than the intestines of a buffalo or the weave of a reed basket—or clay pot which broke as the travois rattled across the plains or a canoe hit rocks in the river rapids. Thus convenience replaced independence.

A way of life unraveled one thread at a time from cultural and technological as well as military pressures.

It never ceases to amaze that the historian believed the musket alone destroyed the Native American nations.

Yet the Native arts have not been totally ignored. In 1969, a Pulitzer Prize for best novel in America was awarded to an Oklahoma Kiowa, N. Scott Momaday, a highly educated, well-trained, most creative man. His masterpiece, *House Made of Dawn*, not only catapulted Momaday into international recognition but exploded into an ironic enigma . . . a "discovery" or "renaissance" of those who had been here all along, alive and creating—a "renaissance" of Native American writers, turning the lights of recognition onto such writers as Leslie Marmon Silko (Laguna), James Welch (Blackfeet/Gros Ventre), Wendy Rose (Hopi/Miwok), Duane Niatum (Klallam), and Peter Blue Cloud (Mohawk), poets and scholars such as John Mohawk (Seneca), Alfonzo Ortiz (San Juan Tewa), and Kimberly Blaeser (Anishnabe).

Listening to Leslie Marmon Silko Telling Stories
New York City, 1979

I take February ice and chill
in stride, enter the subway
to write the various faces
sitting to either side
know children will always listen
as the train shuffles from magic
to Brooklyn

Slowly, visual artists appeared on the scene: Juane Quick-To-See Smith (Flathead), Allan Houser (Apache), T.C. Cannon (Caddo-Kiowa), and Stan Hill, bone carver (Mohawk) among many, many others. Native American culture reached a larger non-Native circle including all humanities and sciences, a culture interested in spirit and language as much as weapon making, ceremony and husbandry rather than the pervading, negative image of the beggar Indian, the extended hand hoping for the white man's gift of infected flour and rotten bacon or "fire water," rotgut, which would bring the people to their knees.

Before this awakening, thousands of books had exotically depicted the "wild savage" of the "new world," his naive spiritual sensibilities, or his bloodthirsty habits and pleasure of participation in hideous tortures. After N. Scott Momaday, truth became self-evident that Native people did not enjoy, celebrate or seek out war, contrary to the propaganda of government, Hollywood, television and cheap Westerns.

It is in the pall of this propaganda that the dawn raid and massacre on the Washita River of 1868 has been misnamed the *Battle* of the Washita.

Battle? Outrageous! It was massacre!

During this massacre, this war crime, Monahsetah was pushed forward under the gaze of General George Armstrong Custer, the Creeping Panther.

Archaeologist

Out of a sandy field
of wild strawberries
he kicked up
an arrowhead,
and his foot bled.

Massacre and Monahsetah on the Washita
November 27, 1868

The bitter cold night hung against the world a thin lining of ice. Even the clear metallic sky hurt to look into—the rising pale moon and stars were cheerless and hostile in their sterile gleam. The general had forbidden campfires and had issued orders that the soldiers leave behind with the supply wagons their extra gear and heavy overcoats, which would be cumbersome in battle.

Now he ordered that not a foot stomp the snow-covered earth in fear that the slightest sound would alert the camp below, over which Custer and his indomitable 7th Cavalry were perched like icicles, waiting in the hungry bite of winter for bugles to blow to call the dawn attack.

No fires, no movement, not even a tin cup of coffee for warmth was allowed the fatigued troops. Was this mad general creating a determining hate to fester in his men against the Cheyenne below within the comfort of their buffalo furs inside warm tipis? If this was his intent, then he met with success. The 7th eagerly awaited the dawn to charge the "red savages," and possibly, in the heat of battle, to warm their frost-bitten toes and fingers.

They would enjoy victory for a moment and happily head back to the comforts, such as they were, at Camp Supply, a tent against the snow, a thin fire against the cold. Killing hostile Indians was one thing, but freezing to death while waiting to pop a frosted rifle was something else.

The Osage Indian scouts mumbled to themselves the futility of this projected attack. They feared that the General Long Hair Custer would be defeated, and his remnant forces would march off leaving them to the anger and torture of the Cheyenne, their ancestral enemy.

A wolf howled on the blank tundra of the plains, and was answered by an Indian dog. For a moment not a breath in the lines was taken. Perhaps the wolf was a scout for Black Kettle. His Southern Cheyenne villaged here beside the iced banks of the Washita River, wending at the feet of the Antelope Hills.

Custer, with his staff, was on a slow incline of the ridge overlooking the valley encampment.

Hard Rope and Little Beaver, his Osage scouts, and California Joe, Custer's head white scout, were with him. A few officers had fallen asleep in the snow piles nearby, in places as much as two feet high. The tinkles of the Cheyenne pony herd bells crossed the stillness of the close night air, heavy with both cold and anxiety.

An icy arm of wind passed over, and soon a light snow fell.

Some of the troops crouched in the banks seeking warmth, while others just stood about grumbling and cursing the "savages" below and their "hard-ass" general in front who seemed inhuman in his resistance to cold and fatigue. They complained bitterly, and leaned against their horses for what body heat they could feel through the animals' shaggy coats already prickly with slivers of ice and covering with a thin veil of snow.

The fierce night wore on, unhurried across the glass of the moonlit sky.

Again the starving wolf howled, and again was answered by the dogs in the village.

This was definitely a complete village with wives, children and the elderly, rather than just a small raiding party camp, which some scouts had predicted. Indians never allowed dogs to follow a war party and rarely women.

The Cheyenne lodges were a good distance off but the soldiers in the front lines on the sloping hill crest could easily see the fires of the Cheyenne camp flickering and sputtering, though unattended, and slowly as the night cautiously passed into the late blackness, the blackness of dawn, the fires dimmed and were at last a spiral of smoke rising to cut the hard light of day.

Custer and his staff, Benteen, Hamilton, Moylan, nervously, agitated, watched the night moon drop away from view, then were pitched into a terrifying darkness only to observe a rocket ease across the horizon. After a great splash of brilliant crimson light, they breathed more comfortably. They had been watching the ascent of the morning star.

Custer's luck would hold. Surely the star was an omen of success and victory. His staff, even the Osage scouts, smiled confidently.

Grey dawn lifted and morning awoke like the burst of a shell, smoky at first, then pearl and pink, milky with streams of pale yellow slanting across livid mounds of snow. The sun splashed brightly over the heads of the tired men of the 7th Cavalry, and cast shadows of a few cottonwoods into the image of thin fingers knotted in the grip of pain.

The sun careened into the chromium sky and struck, blazing, against a gathering of willowy clouds. Soft winds now scuttled amongst the clouds. The morning splendor was barely noticed by the pony soldiers, but Osage scouts, with Hard Rope and Little Beaver consulting with the young general, cried out a song that it was a good day to die.

General George Armstrong Custer belted his saber to his waist. He ordered his officers to their troops and battalions. He made sure the cavalry band was ready to march, ready to play and encourage his soldiers, prod the attack and ring out a glorious victory for this ambitious boy general whose eyes were focused upon the Indian village below, half hidden in the growth of cottonwoods beside the Washita, but a general whose vision pointed east to Washington, D.C.

Without breakfast, without even the warmth of a cup of nourishing coffee, the 7th was ordered to mount, and before sleep and fatigue could be washed away with a handful of snow, the bugle sounded charge and clanged against the brilliance of the very early hours of morning. Instantly the 7th galloped to the village below, the regimental band playing the Scottish airs of "Garry Owen" behind the rushing troops.

The encircled village had been taken by surprise and wiped out before many of the morning hours had passed. Warriors were dead on the bloodied snow, captives taken, lodges burnt, and winter supplies as well, and all the Indian ponies shot, probably a foolish mistake. Black Kettle and his elderly wife were dead in the waters of the Washita River. Women and children were butchered, ancient men dead and scalped, young braves slain and mutilated.

The peaceful village had been asleep at the attack, but the rifle blasts had brought them from the lodges naked and unarmed.

Monahsetah held her baby to her breast under the Buffalo robe.

As long as Bird Girl was nursing, she would not cry out and alert Custer's soldiers to this small bundle of humanity hiding in Black Kettle's tipi. Monahsetah loved her baby more than anything else, and at this moment she wanted Little Eagle back. She wanted his quiver of arrows and even his warm body. As much as she hated him, she loved him more.

If she survived this day, she would find him.

Monahsetah listened to the rifle fire and the cries of the wounded and the families in mourning. She knew women were gashing themselves and cutting their hair.
      She recognized the sounds of mourning as distinct from the cries of the wounded, or those of running away or calling to gather their families. She listened as the voices of the Cheyenne faded and the voices of the English tongue troubled the air, along with laughter and whooping. Overcome with terror, she felt that she would prefer the tipi be burnt. For herself alone, yes, that the tipi would burn and bring her to a quick end—but for Bird Girl she must live.

She smelled her daughter's hair and listened to the comforting sounds of nursing.

In the distance, one of the rifle shots struck her brother, Hawk, and killed him instantly.

One of the shots struck her father, Little Rock, who was leading a group of Cheyenne to safety. Monahsetah heard these two shots but did not recognize them as special among the din.

Elliot, with his contingent of fourteen troopers, had followed a small group of women and children chaperoned by three braves, one of whom was Little Rock. Elliot trailed them to the river, upstream from the village where at the edge of the Washita, Little Rock was killed, and his vermillion blood bubbled in the cold waters. Before dying he had managed to lead his small group of helpless ones to the aid of the other villages of Indians beyond Black Kettle's encampment.

The warriors attacked, saved the frightened women and children, and wiped out Elliot's fourteen soldiers.

Custer ordered his own dead to be buried, and with a strong heart dashed off for another battle, and another victory or at least another confrontation of words if not the red blood of an Indian.

Custer had won a "glorious" battle.

His name would spread to the eastern capitals, to Washington. His star, like the brilliant morning star that had exploded and splashed the sky before the massacre, would rise. Custer's luck had brought them through the victory over this sleeping village of Cheyenne, many now naked and dead on the banks of the desecrated snow.

It was on such a morning as this that Col. John Milton Chivington, the *mashane*, the mad one, had surprised this same peaceful band, encamped on the winter banks of the frozen Sand Creek four years before almost to the day. Black Kettle had thought he was encamped within the safety of the army's protection at Fort Lyon. Nearly three hundred Cheyenne had been massacred.

Now, again, Black Kettle, the "peace chief," believed his people to be safely within the friendship and protection of General Hazen, commander at Fort Cobb, 40 miles off. This great chief who loved his people and their ancient ways of love, life, war and song, would no longer sue for peace with the whites or their distant government.

Horses

The red horses romp
the windy green
disappearing
an echoed scream
into the fires
of the agonized sun
but the bronzed horses
return purely white
the hoofs pounding
the turf of twilight
into the blue horses of night
they charge the range
and come riderless back
riderless the horses come

Black Kettle had received premonitions of the genocide the white government of the good great grandfather was affecting in Washington, and over and again he had treatied away his lands and rights only to find the treaties broken and scattered across the prairies and plains of what was once called the "great American desert" by people who didn't know better. This chief would treaty no more. Only a short time before he had traveled to touch the pen at the council at Medicine Lodge, 1867.

At last his broken lance held meaning as a symbol of submission.

Extermination of peaceful Indians was always an easy thing to accomplish . . . a simple matter for Chivington at Sand Creek, and that morning on the Washita it had been only the blare of a bugle to affect the destruction of the peaceful village of Cheyenne. Custer reported 103 braves and a few women and children had been killed, nearly nine hundred of their ponies foolishly shot dead, most of their ammunition seized, over a thousand buffalo robes taken and burnt with the Indians' lodges.

Custer corralled 53 captives, no males over the age of fourteen amongst them.

His own losses were nineteen men dead and a few wounded.

A lineal relative of Alexander Hamilton, Captain Louis McLane Hamilton, had been shot in the back of the head while riding beside General Custer in the early moments of the morning attack. It has been suggested that the bullet was meant for the arrogant general himself . . . by one of his own men.

After the dawn massacre, there were great feelings of triumph in the ranks. Soldiers took many scalps from the dead and trophies such as beaded goods, lances, and war bonnets.

The dead counted and the village totally destroyed and in ashes to his satisfaction, Custer viewed the prisoners, the women and children. Most were either very young or very old, the helpless ones, the people so impeded by age that they could not escape out onto the snow-covered plains or downriver to the camps of friendlies or across the Washita and into the Antelope Hills, or find refuge within the villages of the Arapaho or Kiowa encamped further downstream.

But among this large group of frightened prisoners, there were a few young girls who interested the officers. Custer looked them over, hurriedly, for off in the distance there was still firing, the men under Major Joel Elliot who had been sent by Custer to draw off fire from possible snipers.

He must clean things up quickly and get out of there, return to Camp Supply, and announce the victory, that he had won a major battle with "warring hostiles."

Custer chose not to recognize that this encampment was a band of peaceful Cheyenne and weak from both cold and hunger with many of their young warriors out scouting for stray buffalo or deer. The general was absolutely delighted he had caught them, literally, "sleeping."

As he stood looking over the prisoners, a light wind played in his long blonde curls falling to his shoulders, Custer's most distinguishing mark, a characteristic that emphasized his defiance of rule and his impulsiveness, and that would spread his name across the Nations of the plains to the outer reaches of the country and the so-called civilized world.

After the Washita Massacre, his name, Long Hair, would be spoken in spit in the villages of the Cheyenne and Lakota Sioux, spoken in fear and hate. He pulled off his hat, and shook the blonde curls loosely in the breeze, his saber clanking against his thigh. Already he was contemplating the written report to General Sheridan, his superior officer, and how he would parade his gallant troops before the commanding general.

The Indian women prisoners keened for their dead, their wounded, the tremendous losses. They openly wept and gashed their arms and legs with their fingernails or a sharp stone found by their feet. They wailed and cried and yanked off locks of hair, and tore off what ornaments they possessed and threw them into the banks of snow.

They would be as poor and wounded as their dead, their men who would be left frozen and unburied on the plains for the wolves to discover and devour.

Figures Before Dawn . . . and After

ghosts, many ghosts
       moving
across the whispering sands,
       deserts
of the western plains

ghost of Roman Nose
       Yellow Wolf
       Black Kettle
       Monahsetah
       babes tugging on the nipple
            for a sip of milk
       babes on the point
       of a bayonet;
       teenage girls with bodies
       cut open
       to winter winds
       of time

wives crying in shadows
twitching in cold waters
       of the Washita
Custer cursed and spat upon
knowing he too would fall
and become one more ghost

Shivering from cold and terror, the captives huddled together, many half-naked as they had been roused from sleep, they huddled together in a great mass, warming each other's feet and hands. Like specimen of bacteria, they writhed and wove a design of fabric of pain and misery.

They feared that this Long Hair Custer would turn his guns upon them as he had upon their captured ponies.

Custer thought to himself, "We see him as he is, a savage in every sense of the word," repeating silently words that he had written for an eastern publication. "Cruel and ferocious . . . wild beast of the desert." He could have been writing of himself.

Black Kettle's sister, Mahwissa (Red Dress), understood what was about to happen. She pulled Bird Girl away from Monahsetah and gave her a stern look.

"What are you doing?" Monahsetah gasped.

"You'll see, stupid girl, I'm saving our lives!"

Mahwissa handed Bird Girl to Monahsetah's grandmother, Tovish, who put a little honey on her finger and let Bird Girl suck on it.

Mahwissa knew that the officers would soon choose among the young women, and she believed that the best hope for Monahsetah and Bird Girl to survive was for Custer, the white chief, to choose her. They might all be saved by this.

Mahwissa rushed forward to gain Custer's attention.

Her ragged blanket pulled loosely about her figure, a spatter of dried blood on her hand that clutched the folds together, she gathered together what pride and fearlessness she had left to command. Her braids had been cut and consequently her hair straggled around her serious face, and a slash on her right cheek suggested she had lost loved ones in the foray that morning.

"Savage customs disqualify him from exercise of all rights and privileges, even those pertaining to life itself," Custer thought.

There was no time to waste in listening to this woman in mourning, but his swarthy interpreter, Romero, suggested that the general give her a moment or two, as she was the sister of the dead chief, Black Kettle, and perhaps had the power of the band now. She would certainly be the leader of the captives.

As Mahwissa approached, Custer, looked about as if for an aide. He pawed the snow at his feet and shot nervous glances to the crowd of captives. Then cheerfully, arrogantly tossed back his yellow curls as if to defy this strangely powerful woman, and he stood straight, one gauntleted hand resting on his saber handle, the other gallantly holding his hat at his side. He squeezed a smile, his eyes merrily playing games with the scene before him. But as if agitated, he snorted once, cleared his throat and made ready to receive the captive woman.

Mahwissa told Custer that she was no ordinary woman of the tribe, but that she was the sister of the head chief, old Black Kettle, who had fallen to Long Hair's guns the moment the attack was made. It was her blood brother who had first heard the troops advance and had called out to the peoples to take arms to defend themselves, and for the helpless ones to flee to the river.

She made signs with her hands to the four cardinal directions, to that which is above, and below and to the right and that which is to the left. She dug into the snow until she could gather a pinch of earth and, crumbling it within her clenched fist, then blew it to the winds.

General Custer wiped off a smirk. Surely she would bring a Peace Pipe from under the folds of her torn blanket and offer it to him as she had just now given him the right to her lands.

Calmed after the ritual, she once again commenced her harangue against her brother, Black Kettle. It had been her brother who had leaped from his lodge and fired the first shot in the attacking troops and had uttered the first war cry of the dawn. He and his old wife had been wiped out almost immediately and now lay heaped in a pile side by side at the river's edge.

The Washita flowed with their blood.

.

No more would he lead his angry warriors against white or bluecoat. For many moons she had advised him against his depredations on the *vehos*, had begged him to make peace with these new friends. Had not Long Hair himself just now told her that the army is the Indians' best friend! Now this foolish old man was dead and could no longer lead the people into war. Perhaps now there would be a semblance of peace in their hearts and fear would wither like the autumn grasses on the plains.

She harangued for ten minutes—to Custer's impatience—blaming every chief and sub-chief in the band for this disaster. Custer grew weary of her ramblings, exhausted from the long march across the night and from the battle itself, and yet he listened because there still fired in his imagination the glory of victory, the vanquished, and how he would tell this incredible tale of the conquering hero and his troops to Sheridan.

She was telling him only what he wished to hear: that he was noble and glorious in victory, that the savage Cheyenne were despicable and base in defeat, that they had brought this on themselves. He anxiously awaited to report this to his commander.

Romero advised the young general that the old woman was playing up to him, that she was as dangerous as any warrior in battle and she would as gladly lift his scalped hair as to take his meat for food. Custer gave a moment's thought to this advice, and though eager for further glory and fawning admiration from whatever quarter, he decided that Romero was probably right in his estimation, and perhaps he might not pay the passionate woman too much attention.

He scrutinized her hands for any sharp knife which she might well be hiding, holding in shadows for the moment to plunge into his flesh. He brushed her off with the idea that she was merely attempting to ingratiate herself and the other captives. She wanted only to save her hair, or life, and that of the others in the writhing huddle of human flesh.

Custer held his hand up, about to dismiss her from this interview when she turned and beckoned a young woman to step forward from the huddle of prisoners. Monahsetah turned aside to allow the girl to pass closely, then pushed her gently to the general.

Monahsetah nearly fell into Custer's chest.

She pulled her dignity, what she had left, about her and stood before Custer. She was barely twenty, beautiful, composed but in shock. Custer believed she was closer to seventeen, and he mistook the calm on her face as innocence when it was actually sorrow and bewilderment.

There were few traces of drudgery displayed on this girl. There was almost a regal sheen to her countenance. She looked down at her moccasins then at Custer's hands. She woke up to what was required of her if her life and Bird Girl's life would be spared. She showed little fear before this white chief, the Long Hair. She showed no anger, either, nor desire for revenge, only the innocent face of a lovely young woman.

She struggled not to look around for Bird Girl, but she piqued her ears for the sound of Bird Girl's muffled whimpering, the high sounds of a mockingbird looking at a snake.

Mahwissa continued in her harangue against the Cheyenne men, blaming them for all of this misery, playing on Custer's male ego. Occasionally, the girl's eyes would lift to glance at Custer, studying his attitude, or her soft eyes would fasten their gaze upon Mahwissa.

Again Custer thought to himself words that he had recently written pertaining to the plains Indians: "stripped of the beautiful romance . . . transferred from the inviting pages of the novelist we are compelled to meet with him . . . ."

Custer shook his head and stared at the ragged woman, "*Mah-wis-s*a, wild beast of the desert."

Romero repeated in English symbols: *Mo-nah-se-tah*.

The girl's name was translated: Young-Grass-That-Shoots-In-Spring.

A lovely name for a lovely face, Custer thought, and made a stiff bow to the girl.

Custer would later write about her in *My Life on the Plains*:

> *Little Rock's daughter was an exceedingly comely squaw, possessing a bright, cheery face, a continence beaming with intelligence, and a disposition more inclined to be merry than one usually finds among Indians. She was probably rather under than over twenty years of age. Added to bright, laughing eyes, a set of pearly teeth, and a rich complexion, her well shaped head was crowned with a luxuriant growth of the most beautiful silken tresses, rivaling in color the blackness of the raven and extending, when allowed to fall loosely over her shoulders, to below her waist.*

Custer's description bears the tone of high romantic fiction and something of the noble savage, where she appears to serve as a symbol to Custer as much as a human being, as if the personification of Nature, perhaps, approving, smiling back at him, forgiving him for his trespasses. A little wish fulfillment, perhaps.

Custer looked upon Monahsetah fondly, took in her complete form and then paused for the Chief's sister, Mahwissa, to continue.

She enjoined the hand of the girl with his, and in her native Cheyenne tongue, delivered a ritualistic speech and benediction, placing her hands first on Custer's face and then the girl's.

Monahsetah's cousin, Kate Bighead, let a chuckle escape at this point, beginning to understand Mahwissa's plan. She stifled the laugh and looked down at the ground.

Custer was off-guard to this spontaneous ceremony. Not sure of what was precisely happening, he smiled somewhat in approval, and held his ground, continuously smiling, almost breaking into outright chuckling, engrossed but certainly a touch skeptical of the woman's actions. He did not move away.

Custer turned to Romero, his Mexican interpreter, who was married to a Cheyenne woman and had a decent understanding of the language. Custer inquired what the woman was doing, what witchery was she performing!

Roaring with laughter, Romero replied, "Why, she's marrying you to that squaw!"

The General blushed. No man could be condemned for enjoying the sight of a pretty face. And no man could be damned for the warm sensations that moved through his blood. She was pretty and dignified, lit with some glow of nobility—and he was lonely.

He ordered Romero to explain to Mahwissa, old Red Dress, and to the younger Monahsetah that he was honored by this unusual presentment but that he was already married by the white man's law, and that under that law was not legally allowed to take a second wife.

Yet he knew of all the frontiersmen and the many army officers who had taken a second wife, an Indian wife, who had lived with them for a time and had sired their children . . . half-bloods that now hung about the traders and the army posts.

Custer smiled gratefully at Monahsetah, as though she had offered him a cup of tea, and held up his gloved hand in benign refusal, but his eyes and his heart said *yes*.

He sought for pieces of hardtack in his pocket that he could offer as a present to the two Indian women.

Mahwissa pushed the young woman, Young-Grass-That-Shoots-in-Spring, toward her new husband. By ancient Cheyenne custom, they were now married, and Mahwissa felt relieved, that their chances of survival had improved.

With a heavy heart and an almost boyish laugh, Custer strode off to his waiting troops. Romero paused, signaling to the Indian women, and shortly followed after his general.

Soon the women were placed in supply wagons for the long trek back to Camp Supply.

Monahsetah was readied for Custer's tent.

Word spread quickly that six miles beyond the bend in the Washita there were large camps of other Cheyenne bands as well as many lodges of Arapaho, Kiowa and Comanche. They would be forming for counter-attack. Custer ordered his band to play and his troops to mount and march in retreat for Camp Supply.

Someone suggested to the impatient general that he should reconnoiter the area for Major Elliot and his command who had been commanded to scout the rim of Black Kettle's village for possible snipers. Custer simply raised his gloved hand and announced that Elliot had probably returned with his troop to headquarters. Elliot's safety seemed of small importance to this conquering hero.

Custer rode triumphantly into the post, the regimental band warming the air with "Garry Owen," his troops dressed with spit and polish, his Osage and Kaw scouts, like autumn leaves, painted for war and celebration and holding high on the point of their lances the scalps of the dead Cheyenne, their bodies left frozen on the Washita banks.

Among the scalps, held like a guidon, was possibly that of the old chief, Black Kettle, which would have been a sensational prize. Later those same scouts held a victory dance and celebrated with the captured scalps late into the night. The fifty-three captives—the oldest male being Mahwissa's son, Little Beaver, at fourteen—were marched, afoot, before the troops, struggling to keep abreast of the mounted command.

Among the women were both Mahwissa and Monahsetah.

Mahwissa had a few minutes to tell Monahsetah how to treat Custer if any of them were to survive and eventually be released from captivity. For Monahsetah, it was Bird Girl's life that mattered most. And she still held hope that her father and brother had escaped the attack as they were seen moving away with a group of women and children. One of the captives claimed having seen Little Rock felled by a bullet, but Monahsetah knew there was still a chance that he was carried to safety by the fleeing Cheyenne.

She would hold this hope for nearly a year.

Their first night together, Monahsetah faked the pain of virginity, and pretended to be naively in love, fawning over Custer, giving the appearance of wanting to stay close to him. His smell was rankly sweet and unpleasant, his beard felt like a tumbleweed against her face, his hands were rough and clumsy, but she endured it all, keeping her daughter's face before her mind's eye. At times during the night, she could hear Bird Girl crying for her mother's smell, warmth and milk. Huddled with the other captives, Grandmother Tovish did the best she could.

There are many forms of strength, and many ways to be heroic.

Upon returning to Camp Supply, General Sheridan wanted to tour the site of the Washita Massacre with Custer to review the scenes of the battle and to confirm Custer's version of events. It would seem that Sheridan was already aware of Custer's propensity for self-aggrandizement, if not outright dishonesty, and among other priorities, he wanted to learn, first-hand, what befell Elliot.

Custer took Monahsetah with him. She had to relive the horror while accompanying Custer and Sheridan on the various routes that the army had followed in surrounding and invading the village, then tracking down the fleeing Cheyenne. They found Elliot and his troops huddled in a circle, naked, frozen, mutilated, the bodies forested with arrows.

Monahsetah could hear the rifles firing and the screams of her people all over again and could see Bird Girl's innocent face.

The Cheyenne who had escaped from the Washita Massacre were now organized around Chief Stone Forehead. Sheridan and Custer would not simply allow this band of Cheyenne to continue living as before. Another massacre was already being discussed. Mahwissa offered to go to Stone Forehead's camp, reasoning that she could convince the Cheyenne to accept the soldier's demands. Mahwissa was instructed to convey that no harm would come to the Cheyenne if they surrendered their weapons.

Mahwissa didn't trust this offer and nether did Stone Forehead, especially after so many of their brothers and sisters had been ruthlessly slaughtered. The Cheyenne were a free people, regardless, and would not bow to the white chiefs. Mahwissa never returned to Custer's camp.

She urged the Cheyenne to escape for their lives, and she stayed with them as the band fled east.

Sheridan decided that Custer needed to track down the surviving Cheyenne and "bring them in peacefully"

—which, more than likely meant, "kill them to leave no loose ends," no witnesses of the Washita Massacre, and no Braves to retaliate in the coming years.

Monahsetah was to accompany him with only Mahwissa's friend, Sioux Woman. Her baby daughter, Bird Girl, remained behind with Grandmother Tovish, her cousin, Kate Bighead, Mahwissa's two sons, Magpie and Little Beaver, and the other fifty prisoners.

Custer pushed as hard as his men and horses could abide, but after several weeks they had still failed to track the fleeing Cheyenne who had escaped without a trace into the pine forests of eastern Texas.

To rest and regroup, Custer's search party camped for three weeks at Medicine Bluff Creek, a Comanche sacred site recognized by all Natives for its divine properties.

A rock cairn atop the bluff was a pilgrimage sight for young Braves on vision quest as well as a place of concentrated power for medicine men to administer healing.

Monahsetah knew that it was wrong for the soldiers to camp on this site, that it was yet another insult to her people—but it was so beautiful to be there, the sheer cliffs rising hundreds of feet from Medicine Creek and the view from the bluffs stretching to the end of the world.

From that height, she could see the points where the sun left and returned to the earth, the original fire in the east and the exhausted fire in the west.

And the same stars that mapped the sky over Cheyenne country, constellated this sky as well.

She left Custer's tent one night and slipped past the night guards to visit the sacred rock cairn atop the cliff. In its presence, she felt that healing was possible, and that these wars would end, must end. She believed her brother and father and Bird Girl were still alive, that everything lost could be restored. And she felt the strength she needed to remain with Custer until this day arrived. She held love and hate in equal measure, and these were her powers.

Custer's smell had become familiar to her, no longer an affront, and sometimes she even felt safe at night when he slept beside her. And he did seem to love her. She knew that he had a *veho* wife, somewhere, but he looked at her like she was the first woman he had ever seen, and sometimes she would turn around to find him looking at her, thoughtfully.

Still, she could not love him, and she would not try to love him. She kept her anger sharp and her smile soft.

Custer was considered arrogant by many of his men. Some of them tried to seed conflict between Monahsetah and Custer by reporting that she was flirting with other officers, especially his brother, Tom Custer, but this only drove the young general to treat her better, to claim her more completely for himself.

Custer's enemies reveled in overhearing the quarrels that would occur in Custer's tent late at night, Monahsetah shouting at Custer in Cheyenne and he seeming to bow to her anger, or his initial anger met on equal grounds by hers. She was no meek child.

During the day, Monahsetah listened to the Irish cook's colorful oration; bent to her work, Mrs. Courteney gave her opinions and family history to anyone who would listen, and Monahsetah listened carefully. She hoped that learning English would help her to gather tidings of her Cheyenne people back at Ft. Hayes, and Bird Girl most of all. She may even be able to intervene on their behalf if she could communicate effectively.

Custer's officers often stepped into the tent to speak with him in the evening in respectful, quiet tones, as if discussing matters of some importance. Monahsetah strained her ears to understand what passed between them. When Custer wasn't around, she overheard his men talking about her and laughing. They used the name "Sallie Ann" which Tom had given her, an "American" name.

She increasingly understood Custer's love language and comments he made about her to his officers. He was proud of her, and protective as well, but he sometimes treated her differently around his men, as if he was suddenly reminded of his enmity toward all Indians, and that she was one of them.

During the three weeks at Medicine Bluff, a child was conceived between Custer and Monahsetah. She knew right away, and hoped it wasn't so. On the other hand, a child is always a beautiful thing, and Bird Girl would have a companion.

On March 2, at the first sign of warming weather, the soldiers set out once more in search of the Cheyenne.

Monahsetah was asked to look at a site where the fleeing Cheyenne had camped some time before, and to tell Custer's men what could be discerned from the remains. She studied the campsite for a long time without saying a word. Her heart raced, as she knew her brother and father must have left some signs of themselves. She recognized the Cheyenne way of arranging wood for the fire and noticed one fire where feathers had been burned, which was a habit of Little Eagle's. She counted a number of horses by the distinct prints they left and tried to imagine who remained alive. Her face betrayed nothing, as the soldiers followed her from point to point.

She misdirected Custer about what she saw, reporting that twelve lodges had camped on the site and had moved east two weeks before, when, in fact, she knew that it was only a hunting party on horseback that traveled east, that the whole camp set out together in that direction but soon veered southward, crossing a stream and continuing south and west. And it had been three weeks since the Cheyenne departed from the site.

Custer mounted his horse and drove the soldiers east in hot pursuit, following the tracks of the hunting party. The troops rode hard each day, expecting to overcome the slow-moving band. They were able to track the horses all the way around in a loop and eventually to the main Cheyenne camp on the Sweetwater River.

As the soldiers neared the village, Sioux Woman escaped, traveled through the night, and warned the Cheyenne before Custer arrived. They were ready to meet the *vehos*.

Stone Forehead, the Keeper of the Sacred Arrows, invited Custer to smoke a pipe with him. Monahsetah was present when the offer came, and insisted that Custer accept rather than plan a surprise attack as some of Custer's men desired. Custer relented, offering the excuse that there were two white captive women hidden among the Cheyenne and that an attack would endanger the women's lives.

So Custer met with Stone Forehead to smoke a Peace Pipe. The chief spilled pipe ash on Custer's boot and muttered a curse in Cheyenne that if Custer ever again attacked the Cheyenne he would be struck dead at once by the Everywhere Spirit. Custer wrote about the strange incident that night in his journal, but he did not understand the curse, and would not have believed it anyway.

Custer needed a way to avoid war and yet to save face, to give the appearance of a victory after tracking the Cheyenne this far.

Custer did win the release of two women captives, with Monahsetah's help, and he did secure a verbal agreement that the Cheyenne would travel to live on the reservation in Oklahoma as soon as they had rested their horses. As leverage, he reminded Stone Forehead that he had many prisoners at Ft. Hayes, including Mahwissa's sons.

Monahsetah went back and forth between Custer and the Cheyenne to work out this compromise. The Cheyenne believed she was trying to help Custer, and the whites believed she was loyal to the Cheyenne. Regardless of distrust on both sides, Monahsetah saved the Cheyenne and many of the white soldiers as well.

It was a tense standoff in which Monahsetah played the role of intermediary and peacemaker, staying close to Custer and reassuring the Cheyenne.

Custer's soldiers encountered more Cheyenne Braves than expected there, reasoning that a battle would be won but would result in many losses among the whites. This calculation was augmented by Custer's deepening relationship with Monahsetah in preventing further bloodshed. It's quite possible that Monahsetah's love story with Custer saved many lives on the Sweetwater, whole generations that now, unknowingly, owe their lives to her.

Custer turned back toward Ft. Hayes in western Kansas.

On the journey back to Kansas, Monahsetah's pregnancy was beginning to show. Custer was joyful for a few hours, then contemplative and moody until he had decided what to do. He would release her, alive, along with her fellow Cheyenne. They were witnesses to the Washita Massacre, but no one would believe their stories, anyway, and he could no longer bring himself to kill her people.

They would be sent east and south to the new Darlington Agency on the reservation in Oklahoma where they could live out their lives. When the group reached Ft. Hayes, Custer pretended that he had no relationship with Monahsetah whatsoever.

Monahsetah wept when she took Bird Girl into her arms.

Her infant daughter was terribly malnourished and had a vacant look in her eyes. Her grandmother wept beside her, explaining that she would not eat the stale or spoiled food given them, even after they softened it for her in their own mouths. She would only suck on what little honey remained to them until even that was gone. They had no young mothers among them to offer milk. Monahsetah hurriedly pressed Bird Girl to her breast, but her milk had dried up, and Bird Girl's weak sucking motion at her dry nipple broke her heart.

On the third night at Ft. Hayes, Custer broke down and took Monahsetah back into his tent. She was not so receptive this time, and neither of them felt the old connection. Monahsetah thought only of her daughter. By late morning of the next day, Custer's wife, Elizabeth, made a sudden visit to the camp. She had heard rumors and had come all the way west to check on her husband and to protect her hopes for his political career in the east. He heard her voice inquiring about him, and he quickly ushered Monahsetah from the tent, trying to hide any evidence of her.

Arriving and Leaving

A faint hint of gardenia;
a scent of deer hide;
a brush of face powder . . .
a touch of bear oil . . .
if there remains time.

Elizabeth Custer . . .
            has arrived;
Sallie Ann/Monahsetah
            must shortly depart,
cross the plains to half-live, half-die.
Elizabeth will take her wife's chair
            at the table.
Sallie will bag a squirrel in the woods,
            then bear her boy-child
            with a stick between her teeth.
Elizabeth will hold court
            in Washington,
but Sallie will disappear
            from history.

She Crossed the Plains

A whiff of old lady's perfume . . .
a shadow against the tent
the whistle of a lady's skirt . . .
and she was there beside her man.

Rustles in the tent: English and
Cheyenne whispers of "go, go Now"
A young girl hustles out the tent,
her hands holding the bump
at the belly, sadness in her eyes,
and fear streaming down her face,
her grip on a leather satchel.

Who is this Indian, this girl??
I demand to know. Had this
happened before? He can't
be trusted when he is alone
with his troops out here on these
dark nights in the tent. Probably not
even Tom, his brother,
can keep these hussies away:
tramps . . . washer women, camp
followers, and now, now Indian maidens.

The captive Cheyenne were released, exhausted, sickly shadows of themselves. They set out on foot from Ft. Hayes in Kansas to trek to the newly created reservation in Darlington in Indian Territory (Oklahoma). Custer barely glanced at her, so that Elizabeth would not know how much he was thinking about her. Monahsetah had her papoose on her back with a baby alive inside of her just beginning to show. Monahsetah's milk was not coming back, and Bird Girl remained at the edge of death. They walked through predawn light, rested in the shade through the heat of the day, then walked for several hours in the evening. Mahwissa's sons were the closest in the group to warriors, at age 14 and 12, and they proved energetic and resourceful as hunters and scouts. The only Cheyenne who didn't make it to Oklahoma was Bird Girl. She succumbed the day before they arrived.

At first Monahsetah did not tell the others but continued to carry her baby.

The day of their arrival at Darlington, there was much weeping and embracing. None expected to ever see the others again. And they were eager to learn who had survived and who had not. Only then did Monahsetah understand beyond all doubt that her brother, Hawk, and father, Little Rock, had been killed on the Washita. But there were many still alive. Some she saw lying dead were now standing. Some she last saw singing and joyous were now dead.

Little Eagle could not restrain himself. He embraced Monahsetah who returned the embrace with both arms, burying her head into his chest as if no distance had ever come between them. He looked upon Bird Girl for the first time, in death, and his sorrow overwhelmed him. They were soon reunited in marriage.

When Yellow Swallow was born that winter, Monahsetah allowed herself only one week to love him and care for him. She would suddenly wake him up at night to be sure he was still alive, and on more than one occasion, she was seen rocking and nursing him with whispers of *Bird Girl* and *daughter daughter*. Other times, she refused him her breast and left him crying in his bundle of blankets. She was obviously in great distress. After one week, she passed him to her mother, Skunk Woman, to adopt and to raise.

Named for his pale skin and hair, Yellow Swallow would be a constant reminder of the shame of her union with Creeping Panther. All the captives knew that Monahsetah had been chosen as Custer's consort, and it was generally accepted that Monahsetah enjoyed being with Custer on the trail, that she celebrated the life of relative leisure and the prestige of bedding with the white chief. Perhaps her acting job was too good for her own reputation, or perhaps, envy and anger clouded the perceptions of the other Cheyenne. Bravebear, a Cheyenne warrior, entirely blamed Custer for taking advantage of Monahsetah as an unmanly action, for raping the daughter of Little Rock. He did not blame her at all for what transpired between them, but this position was rare among the Southern Cheyenne.

Monahsetah was too proud to refute this defamation, which took on a momentum of its own, but she did give Custer's son to Skunk Woman to raise. Little Eagle supported this arrangement, so that they could start over, so that there would not be a constant reminder of the pale murderer of the Cheyenne people on the Washita. They would have another child of their own and pretend that it was their first child, as if time had started over between them.

As Skunk Woman's son, Yellow Swallow attended the school at Darlington for Cheyenne and Arapaho Children, founded by a Quaker appointed as "Indian Agent" by President Grant. Yellow Swallow was teased but not abused by the other children. At times, however, the elder Cheyenne could be seen watching him curiously. No one ever forgot his origins, but there was also some awe toward him, a belief that he possessed special power.

What made him vulnerable also protected him.

After a brief honeymoon period, fire returned to the relationship between Little Eagle and Monahsetah. He could not forgive her for having a child with Custer, and she could not forgive him for not forgiving her. She repeated that she was a captive and did what she had to do. It was her duty to win favorable treatment from the whites to save all of their lives. Aside from the dead and scalped, she was the biggest victim of all! She had to bear the child of the enemy! Nothing more need be explained.

Little Eagle pointed to his knee and said, "If you can so easily shoot a man in the knee, why didn't you shoot our enemy in the head when you had the chance?"

In 1871, Monahsetah gave birth to a baby boy. She and Little Eagle chose the name, Wolf Belly. This name would encourage him to have a strong appetite as if Bird Girl's diminutive name had prophesied her death by dehydration and malnourishment. A short time later, Little Eagle left Darlington and disappeared from Monahsetah's life forever.

From this point on, even less is known about this important matriarch of the plains, though it would appear that Monahsetah went on to live an eventful life in Oklahoma.

115

In 1875, she was recruited to help negotiate the release of two young white captives at Stone Calf village. The expedition was led by the same Rafael Romero who had scouted for Custer on the Washita and by scout, Isaac Alfrey, who was living among the Cheyenne. During this engagement, Monahsetah began a friendship with Isaac Alfrey and would eventually marry him.

In the meantime, however, in 1875, she married another scout and interpreter, Joe Jarvis, and bore a daughter named Glenna. The marriage ended soon after, and "Ike" Alfrey began to court her.

When Monahsetah married Isaac Alfrey, perhaps the greatest love of her life, and certainly the most lasting, she Anglicized her name to "Morning" from the Cheyenne variants Mayouzah (Morning Walker) and Meotzi (Goes at Sunrise).

This name might have predicted how many times her life would begin again.

Important particulars concerning Monahsetah's and Yellow Swallow's lives may have been lost to us through certain machinations of Elizabeth Custer. Jane R. Stewart, in her introduction to *Following the Guidon* wrote, "Mrs. Custer never mentions any episode which might in any way reflect discredit upon her husband," and goes on to assert, "It was said that on a number of occasions she intervened directly to prevent publication of material detrimental to her husband's reputation."

Elizabeth Custer survived her husband by some fifty years . . . ample time to disfigure the face of history, perhaps bury information leading to a better understanding of Monahsetah's life story. Mari Sandoz based much of her writing pertaining to Monahsetah and Yellow Swallow upon a letter she discovered in the National Archives. When asked to present her source for documentation, she was at a total loss, for the letter had mysteriously disappeared from the files.

There is only one remaining record of Monahsetah's words ever written or spoken. When her mother, Skunk Woman, died in 1901, a hearing was convened to distribute land to her heirs. Monahsetah, under the name, Morning Alfrey, testified that Yellow Swallow was Skunk Woman's son, that he had died at age 20, that he never married and had no heirs of his own. She added these latter details hurriedly and a bit forcefully, as if there may have been more to the story.

To this day there are living descendants of Yellow Swallow among the Lakota Sioux of South Dakota who claim that, upon reaching adulthood, Yellow Swallow was exiled for being the son of the enemy, or left of his own determination to be free of the stigma, that he traveled north and married into the Lakota nation. Perhaps, the "death" that Monahsetah referred to in court testimony was only a symbolic death. Two of Yellow Swallow's alleged Lakota grandsons joined the A.I.M. occupation at Wounded Knee in 1973 as the Native story for survival and dignity continued, and continues to this day.

Many years later Monahsetah appears in a photograph as a seventy-year-old woman, mother of seven—three more with Isaac Alfrey (Mary, Joseph and Sampson)—grandmother of twenty-one, and blind. In this group photograph from 1915, still every bit as beautiful and dignified, Monahsetah poses with her husband, Isaac, and her son, Sampson.

She passed away in January of 1922.

Custer's Death

Custer's suicidal leadership and death at the Battle of the Little Bighorn (or as the Lakota call it, the Battle of the Greasy Grass) are highly debatable madness that continue to drive historians to graze and surf for truth. Should he or should he not have? Was he ill? Was he drunk? Was it simply a case of absolute daredevil tactics which if successful would lead to the White House that election year of 1876? He was known to travel with his own newspaper correspondents while eyeing the presidency. Victory won at war was definitely an incentive to run for the office, as Ulysses S. Grant had in 1868. Like many generals of his time, Custer sought notoriety and advancement as well as creature comforts. All seemed fair in war, love, and election. It has been securely established that there was a strain of madness, though he might not have been raving mad as certain historians have suggested. He was indeed greedy; this has been doubtlessly proven.

How and exactly when did he die and who exactly shot the bullet or plunged the lance into his life and took his breath and spirit? Was it really the Lakota peace man, Crazy Horse? Or the utterly embittered Chief Rain-in-the-Face who was accused of not only ending Custer's life, but ripping out his heart and eating it pulsing raw as described in John Greenleaf Whittier's famous poem? Ironically, years later, Chief Rain-in-the-Face performed aloud and sold copies of the poem on the stage at Coney Island, obviously proud of Whittier's presentation.

> "Revenge!" cried Rain-in-the-Face,
> "Revenge upon all the race
> Of the wild chief with yellow hair!"

I have thought often about Rain-in-the-Face while looking at a photograph of him in which I think, sometimes, to see his ghost . . . or my face. I feel some clear parallels between us. I sometimes go into a rage, yet, unlike Rain-in-the-Face, I have never stood face to face with a true enemy.

O / Rain-in-the-Face

O
Rain-in-the-Face
Lakota warrior
don't you wish you had
torn out Custer's heart
with your angry hands
and eaten it raw
without salt
as ol' Whittier claimed
in the same poem which you sold
on the Coney Island Boardwalk
between bottles of booze
and starvation
   for home in the Dakotas.

O
Rain-in-the-Face
I've wished a million times
to eat the bloody hearts of enemies
gorging hunger, appeasing anger
as I sell my poems across the nation
from the steps of Greyhound buses,
or in those indifferent halls of ivy
that would be happier if I, too,
   sold at Coney Island.

I've been looking at your picture-
postcard on the wall over my typewriter
for a lotta years
the eagle feather standing in the long hair
the satisfaction on your lips
   as though you were pleased
with Whittier's lie
as though you had eaten Custer's heart
   as it quivered in your hands.

Successful revenge is a good feeling
I've thought this a long time
but who do I want revenge against
            and for what?

Who is my enemy?
I have eaten my own heart many times
and eaten the heart of crow, the heart of the sun
but I wear no eagle feathers, I am no warrior
and sometimes think I have no starvation
            for home
no Dakota lands
            no home
there isn't a bear in the mountains
that would move over and offer its cave
nor hawk which would fit me into its nest
and I have never eaten hawk or bear.

Soon Greyhound will growl me across America again
            to your Dakotas.
            Will I find hearth there,
            a heart
waiting to be torn apart in my teeth
swallowed and digested by belly acids?
Everyday I seem to face a battle
            at some Little Big Horn,
gun shots all around and bloodied faces
spring up from coulees,
war cries and death cries
            assault my ears
and I plunge teeth into warm flesh.

O
Rain-in-the-Face
I understand why you sold the poem
to the hordes milling the boardwalk at the sea
            at Coney Island.

Historian David Humphrey Miller, and others, conjecture that Custer was shot by one of his own men from his command and not a Native scout—that a shot rang out, and an officer in the front lines fell from his horse into the waters of the Little Big Horn. Swiftly retrieved and tied to his saddle, according to Miller, the brigade continued its march to the top of the mound where most historians agree Custer died fighting against the Lakota/Cheyenne defending war party:

> *Just then, at midstream, the unbelievable happened. Custer . . . fell, a hostile bullet through his left breast. No Indian could say . . . whether he died at once or later, after his men carried him up the ridge of the river. The wound, in any case, was mortal.*
>
> *As the troopers splashed to a halt around the fallen commander, Mitch Bouyer quickly jumped off his horse into knee-deep water to keep Custer from going under. A moment later the orderly with the flag crumpled from his saddle. A trooper grabbed at the flag and kept it from falling.*

A similar report of Custer's fall is here retold from his uncle, Jack Lockwood, a dispatch rider at the Little Big Horn:

> *I could see the five companies moving together in line, all abreast with General Custer in the lead . . . . When the troops got about three hundred yards from where the Indians were waiting for them, those Indians opened fire on their general and his staff, and they all fell at the first volley. The sudden attack and the fall of General Custer and his staff checked the rest of the troops and seemed to demoralize them.*

And later, Lockwood reported: "We saw the General fall and the troops dismounted, the Indians coming in hordes."

No doubt, the Native warriors defended their lives and the lives of their women, children and the elderly with all the rights any human being has for survival. Had they not, their encampment and many, many of their helpless people would have been massacred. Though there were some ten thousand Native people in the camp, hundreds, perhaps thousands would have been slaughtered and most likely tortured, stripped, and mutilated.

As, of course, the Native warriors, did to the cavalry dead on the hill.

This is not offered as an excuse for barbarity, but as a fact of human nature. Even the tiniest mouse will defend his hole and her pink babies.

Monahsetah's cousin, Kate Bighead, was also there at the Battle of the Little Big Horn with her Southern Cheyenne people, and (referring to Monahsetah as Me-o-tzi) relates a scene of Cheyenne women preventing Custer's total mutilation out of respect to Monahsetah:

> The Cheyenne women, thinking of Me-o-tzi, made signs. So the men cut off only one joint of a finger.
>
> The women then pushed the point of a sewing awl into each of his ears, into his head. This was done to improve his hearing as it seemed he had not heard what our chiefs in the South said when he smoked the pipe with them.
>
> They told him then that if ever afterward he should break that peace promise and should fight the Cheyenne the Everywhere Spirit surely would cause him to be killed.

Kate Bighead continues with her testimony:

Through almost sixty years, many a time I have thought of Hi-es-tizie
[Creeping Panther] as the handsomest man I saw in the south.
And often I have wondered if, when I was riding among the dead
where he was lying,
my pony may have kicked dirt upon his body.

Reno Hill, Little Big Horn
June 25-26, 1876

Seven fires form a sacred hoop . . .
villages circled by people's hands . . .
not so easily torn apart
by bullets' teeth or cavalry charge
though blood still waters grass.
Reno's retreat buried his dead;
Custer's greed ate his flesh,

and his bones and the bones of his men
whimper in the dark as dogs.
Sitting Bull's children flower in spring;
antelope graze these very hills;
fox sniff out mice and loco berries;
wild stallions foal colts
that will prance upon this monument.

Blood enough was spilled . . .
"It was a good day to die" . . .
White Bull sang and Crazy Horse.
The war that was lost was won.
Seven fires burn and form
a sacred hoop of people's hands.
Drunken Reno; Custer sired
no white children.

It has been reported that Custer was discovered dead with his 245 men, dead and scattered around him naked. Some reports claim that he was badly mutilated along with the other men in his command . . . too ugly to graphically retell.

Other reports were that he was found naked but with only two mortal wounds to his body—one in his ear as if an awl had pierced the eardrum and one bloodied wound in his chest—a version expressed by Mahwissa, wherein the chest wound had proved fatal, and that the awl was driven into his ear by the hand of friends of Monahsetah, that they breathed through the awl to Custer's spirit that the next time he came to a Cheyenne camp he would listen to what their chiefs had to say and remember that the Cheyenne were the true tenants of the Great Almighty and held the right to the plains and the buffalo which the whiteman was slowly murdering, both Mother Earth and her animal life—that Custer should have retreated to his own camp and left them in peace.

Monahsetah and Mahwissa both understood Stone Forehead's curse of spilled pipe ash on Custer's boot, and they knew that he had been warned.

As a tool of "women's work," the sewing awl is perhaps gendered revenge for all female captives who had been sexually violated by Custer and his soldiers, the awl inserted into Custer's ear as a kind of reversal of rape, a forced intercourse enacted against Custer. Despite the awl puncture to his ear, the fact that his body remained largely unharmed may be evidence that Monahsetah felt some lasting sympathy for him, that his body was not desecrated out of respect for her feelings, or for Custer's being the father of Yellow Swallow whom they now recognized as Cheyenne. In one version of history, Monahsetah actually stood there above him after the battle. All of this is cloudy and perhaps irretrievable from the past.

After the death of Custer, Monahsetah faded into the gauze of history and obscurity. Historians lost interest in her for nearly a hundred years as no longer important to the drama of the American West, merely a footnote to the Custer legend.

Monahsetah was not honored by the Southern Cheyenne who had been relocated to the Cheyenne/Arapaho reservation in Indian Territory along with Mahwissa and their surviving family members. Most Cheyenne do not admit to recalling Monahsetah's name or whereabouts such as where her grave is situated or exactly who her descendants are or where they might be found.

Her elder cousin, Kate Bighead, claimed that Monahsetah mourned for seven years for Custer, that she bore no son by him but that her actions showed love for him and disloyalty to the Cheyenne. These rumors are contradicted by the body of evidence, but the embittered nature of the misinformation reveals how some Cheyenne may have come to view Monahsetah's role in the bloody saga of Custer.

It may well be that, like the "Lily of the Mohawk," Tekakwitha, Monahsetah was judged to be guilty of betrayal and deserving of the ignoble omission from the Cheyenne book of history, the winter Count/Calendar. She had marched across the Texas Panhandle with Long Hair (Hi-es-tsie), Yellowlocks, Creeping Panther, George Armstrong Custer, had been his lover (or wife), and according to many, had helped him to scout out her own people without knowing whether he planned to kill them or offer them peace.

And perhaps she confessed in her inimical way a certain attachment or love proven at Little Big Horn when her friends did not mutilate his prone and lifeless figure with the sharp knives they carried—and if they had no knife, that they decided not to use whatever rocks they could find or even their own teeth to tear the corpse of this enemy to shreds. If they indeed failed in this obligation, whether fairly or unfairly, the whisper did nothing for the survival of the people into the seventh generation.

Why would the people remember and honor Monahsetah? Why should her ghost be hunted and dug out from the grave and re-adorned with the trappings of life and custom? Why should prayer feathers and ribbons be placed at the gravesite?

Monahsetah, Me-o-tzi, the enigmatic Cheyenne woman, Young-Grass-That-Shoots-In-Spring, not only deserves but demands new investigations and remembrance from things past, because she was there, lost everything again and again, but survived. She left no note saying she was in love with this boy general; she left no word saying she had traveled willingly with the killer of her own people.

Perhaps Monahsetah had been dragged by her braid to scout for Custer.

When I listened for her voice, for nearly fifty years, this is the story I received, that she misled Custer, that she negotiated peace and sacrificed her own body to preserve many lives, that she remained a loyal Cheyenne to the end. She did not kill Custer in his dark bed, but she may have taught him just a little humanity. And she did not raise his yellow haired son! Perhaps, she has been vilified unjustly, as was Pocahontas, Sacajawea, Molly Brant (Tekonwatonti), Mary Jemison, and Unice West, all women who played major roles in this great and outrageously tragic tapestry that records the birth spasms of the United States of America.

Perhaps the whole love affair is just a myth, or perhaps dire truth. Custer knew and few others. Few notches were left on the cottonwood signposts. But the markings remain on Turtle's back whether we know how to read them or not. A ceremony of honor is in order: placing a prayer stick into the earth to commemorate the life of this Cheyenne woman who served an important role in the epic of the "opening" of the West and of the gray skies over traditional Native lands.

Let this poem be our prayer stick, for Monahsetah and for what continues. By Cheyenne poet, Lance Henson:

The Cold

what remains of summer
is hidden in the memories
of crows
in our sleep their shadows
inherit us
we pass the transgressions
of our selves
we sit on the cold mountain
among the lonely wolves

And I will offer a song, words that have just now begun to sing in my head, for Monahsetah:

New Song

We are turning
          eagles wheeling the sky
We are rounding
          sun moving in the air
We are listening
          to the old stories
Our spirits to the breezes
          the voices are speaking
Our hearts touch earth
          and feel dance in our feet
Our minds in clear thought
          we speak the old words
We will remember everything
          knowing who we are
We will touch our children
          and they will dance and sing
As eagle turns, sun rises, winds blow,
          ancestors be our guides
Into the new bloodless tomorrow.

BOOK II

ON TURTLE'S BACK

MARKINGS ON TURTLE'S BACK

from *The Mohawk Creation Story*
                as told by Ray Fadden/Fanetorens

Far above earth was the Land of Happy
Spirits where lived Rawennio, the
Great Ruler. In the center of this
upper world was a giant tree. One day
Rawennio pulled this giant tree up
by its roots.

Rawennio's daughter, who was to be the mother
of the Good and Evil Spirits, came and
looked into the hole left by the uprooted
tree. She saw far below her the Lower World
covered with water and surrounded by
heavy clouds.

'You are to go to this World of Darkness'
the Great Spirit said. Gently lifting her
he dropped her into the hole. She floated
downward.

Far below on the dark water floated
The water animals. Looking upward
They saw a great light, which was the Sky Woman,
Slowly falling toward them.

The Sky Woman had now almost reached the
earth. "We must fly up and let her rest
upon our backs so as to make her landing
easy,' said the chief of the white swans.
Flying upwards, a giant flock of white
swans allowed the Sky Woman to rest upon
their backs. Gently they bore her down.
(Also loons, mallards, and other water birds.)

Muskrat swam deep under water for some earth
for Sky Woman to rest on. He drowned and floated up
but a little earth was found in his clenched paw.

The water creatures took up this earth,
and calling a great turtle, they patted the earth firmly
on her broad back. Immediately the turtle
started to grow larger. The earth also increased.

Opposite my work space, a thermometer hangs, always reads sixty-five degrees, during summer and winter. Beside it hang two photos: one of myself and one of a group of friends admiring a musical concert offered by my good doctor's family, the Waickmans. Between the two photos hangs a turtle shell with pheasant and hawk feathers protruding from the shell's openings. This was a gift from a former student. Road Kill Sculpture, I named it. Tom said it was a road kill and he wished to preserve its spirit. My cat, Sula, has had lots of fun with it over the years, humping up her back at the feathers as if they were birds—scenting the individual smells.

I have always been turned on by Tom's most remarkable gift. It does contain spiritual qualities, this turtle. I feel a strangeness take over my emotions when I look at it hanging on the wall. I feel a calm not only of the passions but spiritual and the physical self as well. Tom's gift has been a pleasure for nearly ten years.

Also hanging from the wall, actually as a curve in the ceiling but next to the thermometer, is a commercially made "Native American" dream catcher given to me by my surrogate son, Dean. His gift was proffered in utter innocence, never realizing a factory can't create the true spirit of a dream catcher. Nor that I would want my dreams or nightmares caught in that particular catch. It is commercial. Actually there are two dream catchers, a small one attached to a much larger one: one for small, less-significant dreams and one for huge important dreams. The sign hanging from the smaller catcher reads, "Made by the Old Ojibwa." Not *traditional* nor *ancient*, but simply "old"—whatever that is supposed to mean.

Why am I sitting here at this typewriter, recording the various items hanging on the opposite wall? I could mention a macaw feather fan I have on the wall. A photo of two friends and myself holding an odd kind of coat. I could write of the two large photos of me taken by Nancy Batagglia and Robert Girard. I could mention the boomerang that my friends, the Brownings, brought as a gift many years ago from Australia. Or a photo of conifers Brett took and offered as a gift. Let alone the cases of books ... some written by friends, some strangers. Or the battery-run strawberry clock from Italy that Elaine and Dennis Malone brought home.

I rarely buy ornaments. If I were to bring things home from trips, they would be rocks from the Southwest, driftwood from the California coast, shells from the Caribbean, twigs of Navajo tea which I used to share with my friend, Rokwaho, or clutches of fresh sweetgrass just ripely cut and smelling of the other world, the spirit world.

The house is hung with literally hundreds of gifts and mementos given to me or collected from my many travels. Coffee mug with a picture of Queen Elizabeth waving to the crowds ... a humorous present from my late student/friend Lorne Simon, the novelist or should I say first, the young Micmac killed on the Canadian highway while swerving to miss hitting a deer. Lorne, Lorne!

The clay chicken that Sasha, my Russian translator, brought from Russia while I was teaching in British Columbia. The stained glass tulip, Wanda, my best friend, made in craft class many years past and mailed as a Christmas gift. The postcard of William Faulkner I brought home from Oxford, Mississippi when traveling there with two Oklahoma students, Thuy and Nick, traveling on a lark to Oxford, then New Orleans and on to the Cajun, alligator country of the Louisiana delta. A wooden owl from Santa Fe, a Scotch bread tin containing dollar bills, a wooden bowl of stones. Silver from Baja, gold from Mexico, beads from Africa, rose quartz from Nevada, a snapshot of Paul Rosado, my neighbor friend in Brooklyn Heights. Oh Paul, the waters over the dam since then, huh!

The NCAA Final Four basketballs from Pizza Hut. Oh yes, I was bitten deeply while teaching at the University of Oklahoma. It was all my chair's fault, George Economou, whose name I shout loud and wide. Until then I had been an intellectual snob. Sports? For idiots! There was a time when I did not and would not own a TV. Now I have two and 450 videos. Shameful. Shameful! What has become of me? I even own an Amdek computer, gift of Scott Eicholz, but not a microwave oven. Never. I hold out on this (or until someone dumps one as a gift). So many, what my darling Aunt Jennie, age 93, would call … knick-knacks.

Why do I hold onto these knick-knacks such as Tom's road kill sculpture, the braided sweetgrass Louie Cook gave me, the macaw feather fan that John Blackbear presented when I visited North Carolina a couple years ago? Why do I keep these dust collectors, which are rarely dusted? The Russian chicken, the Faulkner postcard, the strawberry clock are little pieces of life. Not any life, but my life. Reminders of people, travels, events. They aren't truly knick-knacks. They are more important. They are like pieces of flesh I've extracted from the lives I've come in contact with and enjoyed. The clay black bear from Acoma … the symbol of healing, acquired on a trip with my student, Chad Sweeney, in the same day we visited Simon Ortiz and he told us the Creation Story of the Acoma. The beads which once hung in my hair that a student braided. It was a joy to wear, Gail. Tom's Turtle which I now capitalize. I start the word with a capital T because of the great difference it has made to and in my life, the years I have spent here in the Adirondack Mountains.

How strange when we realize our keepsakes are always of good and happy experiences. Well, not all of mine are of joy. I have in my possession a wisdom tooth. I have a photo in my billfold of a former lover who brought considerable pain to my life and little, little, hardly any happiness or pleasure. Just sufficient for me to remember and keep the photograph. Who am I kidding!

The Turtle is probably the most important symbol of all cultural symbols to Native Americans, especially Iroquois people. It is the very thing upon which we all sit or stand. Turtle is the known world, the mundane, that which we can touch. It is on Turtle's back the water birds placed the figure of the pregnant Sky Woman who fell out of the Spirit World. It was upon Turtle's shell that the generations began. It deserves reverence.

Hence the importance of Tom Riddler's road kill sculpture, his turtle shell with the feathers coming from its mouth and from the far end of the shell. It is on Turtle's back we exist, survive, prevail, to paraphrase William Faulkner's Nobel Prize acceptance speech. Prevail. May I be allowed to repeat this word of incredulous depth of meaning? Yes, even Sula, my cat, held respect for Tom's road kill. She never attacked, she smelled the raw smell of the feathers, yes, but she never attacked. A wise feline. She herself had much of the wild in her. The spirit of the legend, the spirit of the living Turtle killed on the highway continues to hold a respectful if not sacred place on my wall and in my heart and in my spirit. To take nothing away from the symbol of the Christian cross, the symbol of the Turtle may be considered profane by non-Natives, but Indian people honor, rather than worship or deify, this symbol.

The feather Jamie brought back from Baja; a photo of a ten foot cherry tomato plant I grew a few years ago; a long, wood scratching claw I liberated (can't say stole) from a friend's house; a framed Helen Rundel postcard painting of a Long Island scene; several framed poems I wrote; an India ink drawing by the beautiful Native American artist Jaune Quick-To-See Smith, a friend from many years; a colored pencil drawing by Wendy Rose ... the remarkable and gifted Hopi poet/artist Wendy Rose ... of a silly, pony-tailed poet (me) sitting atop a wild strawberry; mucho coffee cups holding pens and pencils; an owl from the Southwest carved from saguaro limb or trunk. These are treasures kept only in my working space and my bedroom. Treasures I should enjoy taking into the grave, or rather up on the scaffold.

Last year while giving a reading for the *River Styx Journal* at Duff's in St. Louis, my long time buddy, the photographer, Adelia Parker Castro, took me to the Barbara Jordon Elementary School where I told stories, read poems and answered questions posed by very young students. Something came up in conversation about death. One child asked how I would be buried. I guess the children thought I would die soon as I was obviously ancient, and true I was ancient to their six years. I responded that I wanted to be buried on a scaffold and proceeded to explain what one was. One charming little girl asked why I wanted to be buried on a scaffold. My reply was so that the animals and birds could eat my flesh. Had I not eaten animals and birds all my life? Then a young lad totally startled me when he innocently, naively inquired, "If the birds and animals eat your flesh, will they eat your spirit too?"

What a question! What a theological question. I did respond but my answer escapes me, being absolutely astounded by such a little boy's curiosity. Long live American school children and long live Barbara Jordon Elementary School if it develops children with such intelligent questions.

This is an "experience" I hang on my workspace wall ... the spiritual memory, much more than knick-knack. It hangs side by side with Tom's turtle shell and the thermometer which always reads sixty-five degrees in shade and in sunlight.

I have been promised that I shall go into the spirit world from a seven foot high scaffold with hawks on my toes, raccoons at my side and bear whispering in my ear. Like the great traditional warriors, I too wish to take my collectables with me onto the scaffold. The Egyptians took their gold, why can I not take my knick-knacks!

This earth became North America, a great island.
Sometimes the earth cracks and shakes, and waves
beat hard against the seashore.
White people say, "Earthquake."
The Mohawks say, "Turtle is stretching."

STEREOTYPING THE INDIAN
Genesis of a Poem, "Stone Throwing"

Stone Throwing

He called out
hey you with the blue eyes
you can't be no Indian

Well, that's what my
father said, too,
to my mother . . .
where did he get those blue eyes?

She just smiled,
and her smile said
none of your business,
and gave birth
to another child
as if to say
it is not the pale of blood
but what
the heart is made of.

Hey he called out
you don't have no
feather in your hair
That's right
I said when I grew
older,
and no rings
on my toes,
either.

What's your Indian
name he asked,
and hey speak some
of that language
It's not a name
or words
that makes a man a man.
My reply finally
calmed his nerves
and I lit my pipe
quietly in the dark.
He left me alone then
probably a little
confused,
but that's life.

I assured him
I could dance
but I wouldn't.

As a Native American, traveling across America or simply walking down Main Street of my hometown can be fraught with danger. No one is stereotyped more often than the American Indian: all Indians are tall, dark, stoic—absolutely humorless—and hide behind a listless smile with the desire to massacre. Such epithets as "Wagon bummer," "Indian wino" and "Indian giver" can still be heard in this country. As a human being, a quarter-blood Mohawk and a quarter Seneca—born and raised in the north hump of New York State—as a poet/writer and a fairly wide traveler of the nation, this misconception, the myth and the stereotyping, remain no less painful and harmful.

First, I am short and the world knows all Indians are brute-tall. My friend and fellow Akwesasne Mohawk, Francis Boots, once jokingly exclaimed during a hearty bull-session, "We're short, Maurice, because we intermarried with white Europeans and their short stature diminished our height." I have lived fairly contented with my shortness. Big guys seem to protect little guys. I have a large nose. Doesn't bother me. It is biologically traditional with Iroquois people—though it seems to bother others, and I am the target of slurs. I have very little body hair, and a neighbor once shouted—"I know now you are an Indian, you don't have any chest hair"—upon seeing me in swimming trunks. This was meant to please me and satisfy his doubt. Probably my most outstanding feature is that I am the proud possessor of blue eyes—thought by many to be attractive. I also smile a lot, and I'm not known as stoic. But it is these eyes that seem to get me into the most troubling . . . to others . . . predicaments. I don't feel that I'm bound to give my lineage every time I meet someone new or attend a gathering. But here and now, as many occasions before, I openly say—my father was Mohawk/Irish and my mother was Seneca/English. And yes, I do have blue eyes.

When I first moved to my present home in Saranac Lake, New York and walked up Broadway one spring afternoon, I stopped to look at various articles in a junk shop. The proprietor came out to the sidewalk and asked if I was Maurice Kenny. I readily admitted, yes. The Mohawk poet, he inquired further. Yes, I replied in smiles. So where did you get those blue eyes? He, of course, knew no self-respecting Indian had such blue in his face.

I admit I was stymied for a quick moment, but soon responded, "You know, that's what my father asked my mother. And you know what, she told him it was none of his business." And I proceeded along my leisurely walk up the street to the post office.

There are times when Americans can be outrageously stupid, ignorant of the piercing pain they cause. This particular man did not pierce me, as I have heard it all before: Do you live in tipis? Do you wear clothes on the reservation? What is your Indian name? Do you think I was an Indian in a former life? Can you cure my cold? Stupid, ignorant, or at least thoughtless questions.

I have been obliged to retaliate through poems, such as "Stone Throwing."

It is easy to understand curiosity. As a teacher, I promote this with all students. But rudeness whether based upon ignorance or not is without a doubt harmful. There is a way to satisfy this curiosity without being rude. As the Anishnabe poet, Diane Burns, once wrote in a remarkable poem attacking stereotyping, "Yes, this is my face. No I'm not Chinese, Spanish, nor Navajo." Today I try to refrain from mocking George Washington's wooden teeth.

Campus Life

The Native students had their own student house
which they worked for funding,
which they raised from ash
brought to life from past ages
and labored over until they felt hands
drop away. A house where both men and women
shared life; worshipped how they
wished whether Native tradition or
Christian Bible. They held
lunches to earn money
to support the house which might
have been called a Long House, Hogan,
Tipi in which they served
Navajo Tacos or fry bread and veggies,
And, naturally, hot salsa. They always sold out.

They lived normal student lives!
Doing what students do:
study, sleep, bat a little ball, sleep;
or throw a hoop, sleep, study a little;
have prayer gatherings, sleep; . . . perhaps
share a hug or kiss, sleep.
Yes, all: Mohawk, Cheyenne, Cherokee or
Creek, Ute, Hopi, whatever tribe,
it was early to bed and wise
to rise for those lads and girls.

But here is the rub:
the drive was often littered
with broken glass of empty beer
bottles tossed and scattered
onto the drive by non-Native kids circling
the house in Chevy cars, more interested
in defiling Native Lands than struggling

a good course in American History
even though some of it was a pack
of lies. Where is the history book

that that could teach the youth how to make
Navajo Tacos for lunch on a Saturday noon, or bat a ball
or dance a Round Dance or Rabbit Dance?
      The Washita still runs.
      Custer blows the Bugle charge.
Yet, the Moccasin footprint remains.

Excursion

I took my History students from MASSACRE 303
on a fifty mile excursion . . . something that might
knock their socks off, put some jelly on their tongue . . .
well, at least be surprised by a bite of human history.
I was teaching in Oklahoma a course in Native American life
and death. Sometimes known as extinction. Truly that was
how it happened when the army
left behind a pile of blood rubbish,
the Massacre at the Washita River. No we did not count
the number of the Native dead, the babies on the bay-

onets; old men with scrotums on the knob of a young
soldier's saddler. Or the horse decorated with tails tied
by a chief's flimsy breechcloth which had hung originally
around his groin.
        I spoke there on the open battleground
where the Washita flowed thin at the bottom of the open
knoll, the very hump of land where Custer stood and had
the bugle blow the "charge." Then they knew that instantly
the fire began and man and child, woman and teen,
dropped to the ground beside a mighty chief never
to rise again.
        My students stood stone in the hour.
One young Oklahoma blonde, pretty girl that she was
rushed up to me holding a handful, a bundle of bones.
She was in honest tears, slightly confused, and asked
in a pitiful voice, are these the bones of a Cheyenne child?
I embraced her, though I knew it was against the rules . . .
No, Pat, these are the bones of a squirrel.

Two days later another student entered my office,
claimed she desired to speak,
in her formal British accent, "concerning
the Washita excursion the Sunday before."
I looked her in the eyes and listened. Tears burst
and she sobbed wildly.

Maple Mush
An Iroquois Recipe

My attitude toward food and cooking was early prejudiced and influenced by my dad who was probably a better cook than my mother. Cooking to him was an art; cooking to my mother was, I think, a way to her man's heart and her children's survival and a household job. A second influence on my culinary ideas and methods was without a doubt the most creative M.F.K. Fisher. Odd but we share initials: M.F.K.: Maurice Francis Kenny. I acquired Fisher's monumental, classic obra, *The Art of Eating*, secondhand in a used bookstore on Montague St. in Brooklyn Heights, Brooklyn where I lived twenty years before returning to the North Country. This was in the late sixties. I paid $6.00 for the pristine volume. A steal. I fell instantly in rapture. Ms. Fisher reinforced the idea of respect not just for the prepared food ... as my father had counseled ... but also from whence food came: venison from the deer, greens from the fields and woods, fish from waters, elderberries from the woods, sap from trees, etc. She spoke of the lovely potato, how to use foods direct from the meadow, forests, rivers. She taught also how to conserve.

It would seem from the above paragraph of this essay that I may well have bad-mouthed my mother's cooking when in all reality she did prepare a marvelous beef stew, made a tasty dumplings of biscuits, and an apple pie you could proudly bring friends home to sample. Her soups were always excellent though her roasts were cooked leather. She made one other dish that to this minute I not only remember with fondness but savor and attempt to duplicate in my own kitchen. It never tastes quite as delicious as hers though friends speak of its excellence. I know it to be most tasty and worthy of a high place in the history of culinary arts.

Does this dish have a name? My mother never gave it one. Perhaps it does. If so, I am unaware of what it has been labeled. My mouth waters for it this very moment, and I may need to leave this typewriter for the kitchen. Lunch is approaching. For lack of a name, let us now simply call this dish "Maple Mush."

Recipe: Maple Mush

2 cups water
1 cup yellow cornmeal
pinch of salt
butter for sautéing, a tablespoon and one half maple syrup (however much is needed for satisfaction)

Bring water to boil; add corn meal and salt; cook until thickened while constantly stirring.

Once cooked remove from saucepan and spoon into a square dish. Chill and allow to stand.

When ready to serve, strip out the hardened mush. Slice into one-half inch pieces.

Slip into a pan bottomed with melted butter and sauté both sides until crisp. (You may need to add butter.)

Remove from pan and while still very hot pour maple syrup over the fried cake.

Most delicious for breakfast or as a dinner dessert. May serve four.

* * *

My mother claimed this to be an old traditional Iroquois dish. However it well may originally have been made with red beans or whatever color.
As time passed I learned to add something else to this cornmeal polenta. I advanced its use to an entree and left out the maple syrup. Cooking the yellow cornmeal in the same fashion though both water and meal may be necessary so the squares do not break or flake. Using leftover spaghetti or sloppy joe sauce, fills a cavity in the meal. Again, fry in butter on both sides until crisp, lifting gently while turning. Serve piping hot with a three bean salad on crisp romaine lettuce. A tasty summer dinner thanks to my mom's creativity and M.F.K. Fisher's influence. This recipe, our blood, the world . . . go on changing.

SHEPHERD'S PIE

As an Iroquois-Mohawk, the first thought is to offer, present a typical traditional Mohawk recipe such as corn soup, corn bread, or some use or other of fresh meat, or I could suggest some more modern recipe such as a sweet drink made from the crushed wild strawberry, or even a favorite dish from my childhood: fry bread with maple syrup or wild honey taken from the bees' tree nest, or perhaps macaroni goulash. Corn soup should be prepared with venison, wild onions and carrots, none of which are easy to come by—neither is the soaked white corn (dried first). Originally, corn bread takes much time to prepare: the pounding of the dried corn to flour and the cooking in a boiling pot of water. Only a master will and can take this amount of time and energy in preparation. And as to fresh meat, well, not many cooks prepare, or diners favor opossum, snake, or raw heart or liver (without salt). Consequently, I choose a more modern dish that both Mohawks and non-Native folks relish on a cold January night at dinner, the famed, though often *de*-famed, shepherd's pie, which was brought to the Americas long ago by the British and was originally made of leftover lamb roast. But as lamb is not the preferred meat in our house, we substitute beef, ground meat, pork, or fowl (chicken or turkey), all leftover roasts.

Surprisingly, but Jeff Smith, the frugal gourmet, does not include this recipe in his book, *The Frugal Gourmet Cooks American*. How more American can you cook! Lamb could also be replaced by venison or squirrel. Fanny Farmer includes this dish in her classic cookbook and I am personally delighted to know that Craig Claiborne honors the shepherd by including this pie in his *New York Times Cookbook*.

For this recipe I have chosen to ignore these cookbooks to rely on my own imagination and creativity which my mother years ago savored with her cooking creativity.

Recipe: Shepherd's Pie

2 cups of diced beef (or pork or fowl)
2 bouillon cubes (beef, chicken or vegetable)
dash nutmeg
pepper to taste
1 teaspoon butter
½ cup of scalded milk
½ cup of white sauce (flour and milk)
thyme, parsley, salt
2 cups water
healthy dash of Worcester sauce
1 cup diced carrots
1 teaspoon of paprika
½ cup of chopped celery
½ cup of kernel corn
1 onion chopped fine
¼ cup chopped bell peppers
8 large potatoes for boiling and mashing

In a large casserole or Dutch oven (without the cover), bring the water to a boil; add bouillon cubes and Worcester sauce; lower flame; add beef; add onion and other vegetables; bring to a simmer; add herbs and spices. In the meantime, peel, boil and mash the potatoes and add butter, milk and nutmeg. Add the white sauce to the simmering stew. Spoon by spreading the mashed potatoes (½ to 1 inch thick) over the stew, leaving a large hole in the center. Sprinkle paprika over the spooned potatoes. Oven should be set at 350 degrees. Cook until the sides of the dish show crisp edges. Serve hot with green peas, a leaf salad, and, for dessert, a scoop of vanilla ice cream topped with dribbles of maple syrup. Serves 4-6 diners.

A menu fit for a Mohawk chief or a British duke, at least.

BETRAYAL BY MEMORY: TEKONWATONTI / MOLLY BRANT

One

As men have tended to be the historians and have focused on male figures of history, few women have survived the exclusive club of the written record. But for Native American women, this omission is even more striking. How many Native women can most people count? On one hand? We remember at least two young women, Pocahontas and Sacajawea: Pocahontas of John Smith and Hollywood fame; the cartoon movie played three weeks in my hometown of less than five thousand people even though I protested with a placard. And now Sacajawea is on the new dollar, in the hands of the millions of shoppers and spenders and jingling in our pockets, though no one knows much about her. And who knows Monahsetah, or Sarah Winamucca, or Wilma Mankiller or Nora Dauenhauer? If you have no recollection of these important Native American women from American history, surely you will not have a clue as to the identity of Tekonwatonti/Molly Brant! Shame, shame on all of us. We know the somewhat mythical figure of Pocahontas mainly because a bad cartoon was hammered out of her life, and if we should happen to be from Oklahoma we might know that Wilma Mankiller was a Cherokee Chief, a strong political activist, a fine memoirist and a bloody fine human being. But the Mohawk warrior, Tekonwatonti/Molly Brant! Scratch your head as if for fleas. You won't find her in the tufts.

Tekonwatonti/Molly Brant was more than just the Mohawk wife of Sir William Johnson and mother of eight sired by Johnson, and sister of the famed warrior/leader Joseph Brant. She was first and foremost a woman, a woman who held her own counsel and often counseled governors and generals let alone maids in her parlor, chiefs at the fire, and slaves in the fields. She was a most formidable woman ... handsome, ney beautiful. It has been said by many historians that she was by far the most beautiful woman of all races in the colonies until the whiteman's small pox caught her. She ran an excellent house, equaled her husband's libido and was a ferocious warrior in battle.

I, Tekonwatonti

I, Tekonwatonti
child of these rivers
girl of this wood
woman-to-be of this house
this bed of branches
gathered for my husband
to be woman of this pot
of mortar and pestle
of fields of corn
brambles of berries
of gathered faggots
to warm his thighs
of breasts swollen with milk
for suckling children
and full of stories for winter nights

pleased to love, happy to birth
honored by a good man
will become, at peace, my mother
whose bones eventually
will be enjoyed by wolverine

Two

Tekonwatonti/Molly Brant was born to Nichus Brant and his wife in a Mingo Village on the southern tier, the border between New York and Pennsylvania. She returned to her home territory as a young teenager, actually to the Mohawk "Castle" in the village of Canajoharie, NY. There she met and soon married William Johnson, who had not yet been knighted by the English Crown. They married only by tribal law/ ceremony and were never married by a justice of peace which would have made the union legal in the eyes of the colonists, later the young American citizens. They remained together twenty-one years, and his career was amplified by her own charisma, loyalty and intelligence. She bore eight surviving children with him. By suspicious methods, he died in 1774, untimely. When the Revolutionary War broke out between the colonists and the British, she chose to follow her brother, Joseph Brant, and fought with the English royalists against the American uprising, never dreaming the colonies could raise either an army or sufficient money to win a war. They did win, so Joseph marched to the safety of Brantsford in Canada.

Molly, her children, and servants pushed into the St. Lawrence River Valley and onto Carleton Island where she demanded the English build her a "house of stone," in which she lived some eight years before moving onto Canadian soil to reside in what is now known as Kingston, Ontario where she is buried in an unmarked grave.

> I, Tekonwatonti
> whisper the sounds of my name
> to the voices of the night and the waters
> that we women, the grandmother of the night
> and my sisters in the fields of the sun
> labor the birthing of generations
> of muskrat, loon, raspberry, tamarack,
> and the differing cries of cubs
> to break open membrane
> and be counted

153

I,
I,
Tekonwatonti, I
no, we
children of these rivers
girls of these woods and meadows
kissed by the warmth of Grandmother Moon
nourished the mouths, bellies of our men . . .
the Great Turtle, Tarachiawagon,
and the powerful giant, Shagadyoweh,
we women dig the flint and smooth the arrow
happiness in our hands
that we, too, community the village
and populate our future

corn whispers the fields
as winds surge the dawn

She lived an exciting and eventful life as political, intellectual and loving partner to Sir William, becoming a legend in her own right. Most of her time was happy, sharing a life and home with her "darling" husband whom she obviously adored even though he was a busy philanderer. His will left wealth and treasure to Molly Brant and to their eight children, but he left the house to his first common-law wife, a German immigrant named Katerina Weisenberg and their one legal son, John, who at the moment of his father's death threw Molly's brood out of the mansion she had built with Sir William. She died in 1796 in Canada at the age of 60.

Three

Get to the story . . .

How did Tekonwatonti, Molly Brant come into my life? We know that my mother had Seneca and English blood. She was a Parker on her mother's, Lona's, side and a Herrick by her father, Frank. My father is a descendant of Eunice West who was captured at Deerfield, Connecticut and brought to Caughnawaga Reservation just below Montreal, Ontario. My mother was a Parker descendent of Eli and Arthur Parker and consequently of Mary Jemison who also had been taken captive and raised in a Seneca village in what is now known as New York State.

The story begins

Story has long ago begun
it's continuous
in the bear robe warming the old woman's shoulder
in the wolf robe on his husky shoulders
in the turtle rattle held in the other's hand
in the eagle's eye, hawk's scat
story has never stopped

My grandfather, Frank Herrick, had a finely tuned sense of the historic. He hunted arrowheads in his fields and back lots. He read history at his fingertips in the fallow fields of history whenever he could. Frank raised his children on a farm on Fox Creek Road in the township of Cape Vincent, NY. The Cape itself was originally a French settlement, and to this day a colonial French festival is held in the village. Off the Cape's shore is Carleton Island in the great St. Lawrence River. In summer with chores finished off, his bible reading for the afternoon completed for that day, he would sometimes herd the seven daughters together, my mother being the second born, into a buggy and horse to ferry them into the village where they would board a row boat, and he would row them to

155

the island for a picnic. This was about the only joy of those early years of my mother's young childhood. There on the island they would scout around, take short hikes, and while on one hike they discovered the remains of an old house, its foundation. Not much left but sufficient remains to recognize a proper house had once stood its ground on the spot. My grandfather, knowing his history, surmised to his delight that this brick and clay had once been the foundation for the mansion Molly demanded the English build, a "house of rock." It impressed my mother enough so that many years later she told me of these island picnics, though I was never given the opportunity nor pleasure of visiting this hump of clay.

the story has never stopped

it is caught in the grip of the Great Law
it murmurs in the song of the singer
the pounding of the drum, the arch of the carver
the cry of every child, the poet's pen
the raised foot of each dancer who touches earth
and moves as the squash vine moves, as wind,
it is the ever-widening circle of the village
and the fire in the house,
the string of fish caught,
the tongues of elk, the belly of moose,
flight of northern geese,
the color of meadows and meadow flowers,
the sweet berries and the bitter sumac . . .

My paternal grandfather, Maurice (pronounced Morris), was a second generation Irishman who married young to a Mohawk woman, Mary West. I know her first name through hearsay. My father and his family who would have this knowledge have all passed. How this odd couple met I have no idea.

My father left home in Canada rather early, a lad of 13 or 14. He set his father's barn afire by smoking behind its outer walls. He said years later he had fallen asleep. He'd been out to a euchre card game and a dance rather late the night before, and consequently fell asleep with a self-rolled cigarette in his hands. My grandfather bore something of a mean streak. My father knew he would be whipped within an inch of his life. He took off for the states.

When a small boy visiting my father's homestead, I soon learned of my grandfather's meanness. He would hold me on his lap, open a fist and show an Indian head nickel. When I'd reach for it, he'd close tight the fist and with the left hand smack me. I learned two things: not to sit on his lap, and never trust him or anyone else who offered a monetary gift. My father's biological Mohawk mother died when he was quite young. Obviously I never knew her, but what she had of time in which to teach my dad, she taught well. Some of my knowledge comes from study and observation, but much of my cultural knowledge comes from him even though he was alive in a time when it was utterly shameful to identify yourself as a "lazy and dirty Indian."

Indianism was not accepted, and he did not accept his Indian blood in public, though I clearly remember him helping and aiding other Native American men and their families when they crossed the border looking for work to feed their starving children in exodus from the reservation. His method was silent, but his altruistic hand was always there, and I remember it vividly.

the story has never stopped

it is the greeting of the morning,
it is the hope for a good mind,
story are clouds, grebes and coots
partridge drumming the earth, loons singing,
and where humans heard partridges drum
it is the flow of the rivers, crystal of lakes
it is this canoe, hollowed and safe for journey
it is the mind of humans, the joy of the child
the journey

Quite frankly, I do not recall my father speaking of Molly Brant. I flirted with the idea for a time, but came to realize that she was probably no blood relation, perhaps a clan relation and obviously a tribal relative . . . which counts greatly. But we were not descended from her as far as I know.

So why my deep fascination with Tekonwatonti/Molly Brant? Only the thin stories my mother and my grandmother might have whispered into my ear of the picnics on Carleton Island. Perhaps, but let me clear the air here, my grandmother was not a holder of the family lore. My mother would know only what her father perhaps had told her and what she remembered about the island picnics. Because of six siblings who she did not see as often as she might have wished, when they did gather for weddings or funerals, they talked over the past: relatives and particularly their father, Frank, and the marvels he invented for their pleasures when small children such as during the boat rides to the island with their father rowing back and forth.

> *to swamp rose, to tamarack, black willow and oak*
> *a rough path through brambles, eryngo, blue flag*
> *and arrowhead; earth wet, bog, rich and dark mystery*
>
> *silver water ripples decades pass to shore . . .*
> *egret tells time in the flap of a wing*

When I was quite small, my father would bundle up my two sisters, myself and mother and take off for his home. We would always stop for a visit with an aunt, Miss West. I do not recall her first name other than Miss. This lady was a seamstress, a scruffy housekeeper who was always about to start spring cleaning but never got to it, and she was the younger sister of my father's mother. No, she did not know of Molly Brant either or if she did, I never heard the name breathed while in her presence. I now have no idea where Miss West lived, where her second floor apartment was located, but I do recollect most clearly that down the street several blocks was a park. I enjoyed wandering down to these greens, and often found boys to play with, especially baseball and other ball games.

On occasion, while at this park I was amazed by an angelic type of voice speaking to me, directly into my ear. Later, I realized that it was most likely Tekonwatonti speaking, her voice. I was to become a poet, not the priest my Catholic aunts expected. Some poets hear and speak to voices, such as Joan of Arc who I have always considered a poet and a saint. Over the years of searching out Molly's biography both in reading and visiting various haunts she visited, I naturally familiarized with her life and listened intently for her voice as Joan listened for the saints and angels. And lo and behold, there was her voice … communicating ideas and scenes that no historian could have written with pen and ink nor heard, as they were decidedly not poets or saints.

> *story has never stopped*
> *a chain of days, nights*
> *following night on bat wings, or moons*
> *it is the eastern dawn, the grave on the mountain*
> *it is the mountain. it is time itself whatever time*
> *may be, it is the budding of the beech*
> *and the falling of the leaf, whistle of the wind*
> *it is toothless old men, or old women*
> *who no longer hear, spittle of the sick*
> *it is the fisher at kill, hawk*
> *the birth of groundhog*
> *it is the fire, this fire flaming*
> *in the pot-belly stove stoked*
> *and the ol' rabbit dog asleep beside it*
> *it is the story of nations, nation*
> *and history and circles of the trees*
> *circles . . .*
> *winter and story move in the ripples*

Years later, I was to frequently visit Akwesasne Mohawk Reservation (St. Regis). One summer I was staying with the poet/artist, Rokwaho, and his family on Cornwall Island on the Canadian side of the St. Lawrence, my father's side. There was to be held a fundraiser for Dennis Banks in Syracuse as he was to return to the Dakotas. We went, Rokwaho, his wife and daughter, Kaherawks, and one other young Mohawk male, Doug George. In the car riding down to the festivities, Doug, knowing I was a poet and had already written the epic story of Isaac Jogues the Jesuit missionary put to death by the Mohawks for tampering with the women's minds and souls, suggested, no rather demanded, I write the epic story of Tekonwatonti as my Mohawk duty. Even at that time I had written one or two poems concerning her life, though I had no plans to create an epic of some 209 pages dealing with her triumphs and tragedies and those of Sir William. It didn't take much cajoling for Doug to make his points and to convince me it was my job.

I spent some twelve years researching her life and Sir William's, people of their society and times and of course the tenure of those times, the before and aft of the middle to late seventeen hundreds. A powerful number of books and papers read, and people interviewed. My good friend, Sara Iselin, edited the book, and my other good friend and wife of the publisher, Elaine LaMattina Maloney, ordered the poems and wrote a chronology. The book was released in November of 1992. The first printing was out of print by January of 1993 while I was on tour under the auspices of the Lila Wallace Reader's Digest Foundation. Molly resurfaced. She was no longer invisible. She had breath if not vocal cords. Shortly after, her persona was filmed in several movies . . . though basically they were both about her husband, Sir William and her brother, Joseph. Perhaps one day some intelligent and creative filmmaker will put her life on the silver screen.

> *my mother is a turtle*
> *my mother is a fish*
> *my mother is a muskrat*
> *my mother is a beaver*
> *my mother is a boat*
> *my mother is a reed*
> *my mother is my mother*
> *and all her parts are me*

Four

Writing the Tekonwatonti poems was an eighth of a lifetime's work and an all-consuming occupation—of love. Nevertheless, I believed that the poems were not *personal* to me, but merely *persona*. Indeed, in this bright venture, a living though perhaps surrealistic experience, my personality would surely disappear into *Molly's* life and times, rather than imagine my own life within her story. And I believed that I had succeeded at maintaining artistic distance until Craig Womak, a young Native American Creek Ph.d. student, critically claimed that the epic story of Tekonwatonti was not as impersonal as I had thought. While researching my biography and looking into the activities of both Molly and her Irish-born husband, Sir William Johnson, and his machinations, Womak found that the book was far more personal than I had ever suspected. His belief was that Sir William was a close cut-out of my father who was both Mohawk and Irish decent, and if Molly was not actually based on my birth-mother, she was possibly the mother I "had always desired." My mother was of Seneca rather than Mohawk blood, but she held no understanding of her Seneca lines. Her thin knowledge of Native culture obviously came via her father who collected arrowheads and other artifacts and eventually donated them to a North Country museum.

> *my mother is a fish*
> *my mother is a reed*
> *my mother is corn and bean and squash*
> *my mother is sumac and smoke*
> *my mother is honey*
> *my mother is a berry on the bramble*
> *my mother is the sap of the maple*
> *my mother is a boat*
> *my mother is the rapid in the stream*
> *my mother is the wind*
> *my mother is a coot*
> *my mother is a bear*
> *my mother is this house*
> *my mother is the fire*
> *I am my mother and my mother is me*

Upon reconsidering Craig Womak's study, I agree that my father shared certain characteristics with Sir William besides whatever blood might be sifting through the veins. They were both philanderers, both industrious and acquired large sums of money and property though both were dirt poor upon arriving on United States soil; both commanded others yet saw that others less fortunate were helped in whatever way needed. They both drank heavily—Johnson, rum and wine; my father, brandy and beer—yet neither considered himself an alcoholic. Both maintained excellent taste in women: Molly was gorgeous and my mother was, indeed a most lovely young girl. Both were in military service: Johnson fought in the French and Indian war and my father, Andrew A. Kenny, was consigned to the army during WWI. They shared great dreams: my father's was to amass money, to trip to Washington, D.C. during the cherry blossom spring, and to fly to Alaska; Sir William's dream was to amass money and as much land as he could travel across, and most likely woo every young woman he met. It has been said by historians of his day that he sired some 200 children. My father was accused of three legal children and one bastard. Johnson was large in body, raucous in voice, near devoid of humility and appeared to thunder across history. My father was fairly gentle unless drunk, quiet though he enjoyed a good political rap session, and carried a heavy stick which struck down most obstacles but was void of thunder. He was a good hustler as was Johnson. They were welcomed in most homes and enjoyed by men even though there was considerable jealousy hovering about from their contemporaries who were less successful in most pursuits. They died too young before they had completed their work on earth and before the dreams had been totally fulfilled. I have long thought my father cheated himself out of his dreams by caring too much for gold, as did William.

Sir William Johnson has been immortalized by his engagements in the history of his young nation. His battles at Lake George did not necessarily defeat the French but did at least drive them north back into Canada, and because of his huge efforts, English is spoken in the land, among other feats. My father has yet to receive his due, his recognition, as Sir William still is not a household word, such as George Washington, his contemporary. Though it was my father who supported my being a poet, at first when a young college student, he urged me to gain a business degree which would help avoid the usual poet-starvation syndrome.

I dream of my father frequently, nearly weekly. He often simply stands there before me holding game, a string of fish, a string of bloody rabbits, a beautiful pheasant. Sometimes he's sitting in our backyard in a kind of beach chair with my stepmother, Anne. He smiles. Sometimes, he is mouthing words, words of congratulations for learning to drive the old Model T he gave me when I was in high school. I rarely dream of my mother who lived to a good age, 82. As I had more time with her, I do not need to recall her as often as my father who died comparatively young. While I was writing a poem in the voice of Molly Brant at the death of Sir William, I did feel true grief and mourning:

Molly at His Death

Kwaaaaaaaaaaa . . .

My hair streams in the river,
chips of my flesh shrivel under the sun,
the nub of my little finger
is buried in the earth with his bones.

Kwaaaaaaaaaaa . . .

I have no arms to hold me
no cheek against my own
no might to protect my house
or the limbs of my children.
Who will hunt for my pot?

Kwaaaaaaaaaaa . . .

Eight times I spread my legs
and gave him his flesh.
Twenty-one years we lay
thigh by thigh under summer stars.
How do I pull grass over his face now?

Kwaaaaaaaaaaa . . .

Five

My book, *The Mama Poems,* won the American Book Award in 1984. I am not content with that collection of poems but it did much to re-establish my mother's role in my life. I have always said her influence was less than my father's, as it was in his house that I tendered my adolescent years. His home remained "mine" until the day he died though I was actually living in New York City at the time of his death. My mother I knew well into mature years, and we were friends. Like my father, she remarried. I was not happy with this union. He was not my ideal of a father, nor what constituted as a good and caring husband. He was rough and rude . . . completely unlike either my father or Sir William . . . who were both self-taught but very bright, good thinkers and planners.

How correct was Craig Womack in detecting my mother's character in Molly Brant! I don't think he hit it as squarely as he did with my father. The two women shared many characteristics but not half as many as did the two men. Molly was first a full-blood Mohawk woman who spoke her language fluently and practiced cultural duties and ceremonies in a traditional manner. Her loyalties were to her husband, her Nation, and her children, probably in that order. My mother's allegiance was similar but she was only Seneca by descent, held no ties, no sentiments and had little knowledge of that culture. She was a voting American woman who had been something of a warrior similar to Molly in the sense that during WWII she worked in a war defense plant, Western Electric in Bayonne, New Jersey. Molly led a party of warriors onto the battlefield and was consulted by generals. Molly was poorly educated in European ways though she spoke solid English; my mother had schooling, read well, and enjoyed reading particularly biographical materials. It might be where I receive my interests in books. Molly was dominant, forthright, strong-willed, passionate, knew anger and often reveled in it with sweet relish; she was demanding, trusted few, was consumed with adoration for William and was as good a mother as the times allowed. My mother was demanding though at times weepy, totally trusting, flirtatious; she was soft butter in my biological father's hands. My mother was usually a good mother, fed us well, provided whatever was needed, but was not demonstrative in her affection—but again neither was my father who never kissed me and shook my hand only once when I drove off to college. My mother also never kissed, never shook hands, but did cry often. Was this "Indian"? Yes. Do not show emotion, or the passion of love.

> *my mother is a fish*
> *my mother is bone*
> *my mother is yarrow*
> *my mother is hawk-weed*
> *my mother is deer*
> *my mother is snipe*
> *my mother is blue heron*
> *my mother is yellow rose*
> *my mother is sprig of mint*
> *my mother is birch*
> *my mother is cedar*
> *that sings in the wind*
> *my mother is cloud*
> *my mother is star*

Molly knew the scene and could track with the best. My mother was terrified of being lost and avoided the wilds, hated water and the summer camp my father purchased. Molly had the tendency to drag her eight children by the hair of their heads if necessary; my mother was inclined to leave us behind with the thought we would catch up if we needed. Molly had one male love for her entire life . . . William. My mother had two legal husbands and another male friend or two after her divorce from my father though she declared abstinence after the 21 years of marriage —the same number in the marriage of Molly and William. Odd! My mother had no leverage in keeping the apron string on my father's leg or wrist. Neither did Molly, actually. The woods were deep and dark and very wide. My mother basically had no political power, unlike Molly who did have power with both her Nation and the Colonists, however my mother served jury duty and on election boards yearly. I'd suppose there is some thin power there.

Molly could not sit in Iroquois council but she could send her message to the chiefs via her Uncle Hendricks. My mother was known to drop tears on a shoulder; Molly was never allowed this privilege nor did she desire it. She was her own confidant; she had few known female friends as with my mother who held little trust in female friends as she had been betrayed several times. My mother, Doris Herrick Kenny Welch, was a hard-working woman, a neat housekeeper, a decent cook. Her specialty was pie and meat gravy. She made very pretty dollies for the bedside table or the cocktail table, the couch arms, and she was a whiz in the berry fields and at the blackberry canes. I would doubt Molly had either this inclination or the time even though there was necessity. Doris Herrick was a total failure as a political consultant, lobbyist, etc. My sisters and I often considered her weak though a good woman, something of a failure where Molly, Tekonwatonti, was usually successful in her engagements.

my mother is dream
my mother is grave
my mother is wolf
my mother is water
my mother is loam
my mother is fire
my mother is wind
my mother is fish
I am my mother and my mother is me

Both women lived across wars: my mother as a young child lived across the first World War and as a consenting adult over World War II; Molly lived most of her life across one war or another, but mainly as a young woman across The French and Indian War and again as a more mature woman across the American Revolution at which time she was forced to flee as a royalist into Canada. My mother also moved during the Second World War, from home in Watertown, NY to Indian Gap, Pennsylvania to Bayonne, NJ where she sat out the war working in the war plant and waiting for her second man to return from the European war theatre. So they shared this disruption in their lives as well as the characteristics of their men.

My mother, Doris Marie Herrick Kenny Welch, ever so great granddaughter of a Seneca family and also an ever so great-grand-daughter of the English poet, Robert Herrick, will, once her grandchildren have deceased, be forgotten through ignorance. Not even my book, *The Mama Poems*, will keep her memory fired, nor will these scratchings today. Molly has been dead since 1796 and has long been forgotten and ignored with the exception that she does happen to be on a Canadian 34¢ stamps and in my book, but I fear Tekonwatonti will not continue her name down through the ages. Sir William has long been forgotten. Unlike Cleopatra, Molly has no Caesar or Mark Antony nor a Shakespeare to keep her altar fire burning. These two ladies are both stuck with me. They probably won't be so lucky to have a young doctoral candidate look them up on the dusty shelves for regeneration. That is the chance they had to take as did I. But we lived, we lived!

Molly

I wish never to live to see
      another war.
I've gagged on flesh
      and choked on blood.
I've seen the bones of my brothers
      float in the river,
smelled the stench of their rot.
My nostrils are clogged
      with powder smoke.
My arms are weary from the
weight of rifles
villages are burned to the ground,
old men pierced on stockade posts.
Women and babies sleep on the
scars of bayonets.
Maggots infest the bed.

General George Washington, town destroyer,
      you have won.

167

Won and accomplished more in your victory
than you ever dreamed.
Our blood is your breakfast.
The flames of our village smoke
        the ham you carve and bring to your lips.
General George, leader of a new
                country,
Our stars are yours now,
but our blood stains your flag.
Remember we were once
        powerful, a formidable nation
now on our knees.
Your hatred controls
        our destiny.
May your nation never know
        this unbearable loss, this pain,
        this exodus from home, the smoking
        earth,
        the sacred graves of the dead.

I bathe in this river to wash
        away the blood of war.
        But no water can
        wash away
        the horrors tattooed
        on my flesh.

I pray I shall never smell
        the cannons of war again,
nor hear the cries,
        nor see the body of a chief
        mutilated by hate and fear
        and greed.

As your stars, General George, rise
        above the many battlegrounds
I want you to remember all those
        who died
so that your flag my wave
        in tribute.

It has been a happy union, beneficial to all concerned to have such interesting relations to seek and to follow if only through years of research. And I thank, indeed, the young Ph.D. student, Craig Womack, for making the connections.

Few of us are remembered—of the billions of people who are buried and those who shall be interred before the end of the world—and who knows if the world will end by any hand other than humankind! This year's famed will be next year's trash burned in the dump. I suppose there is some truth in Womack's deduction, that there is much of the personal in *Tekonwatonti/Molly Brant*, and if one looks deeply, a line of blood to both Molly and Sir William might be discovered, and deeper still, perhaps, a line of blood between all of us on Turtle's back.

> *my mother is fish*
> *my mother is sky*
> *my mother is rainbow*
>
> *my mother is dream*
> *my mother is drum*
>
> *I am my mother and my mother is me*

ACKNOWLEDGMENTS

The author wishes to thank the editors of the following publications in which some of this material first appeared in whole or in part and sometimes in other forms:

"A Creek . . . Ponoehoe" was first published in *Les Oublies*, 1974, Ottawa.

"Stone Throwing" first appeared in *Clockwatch Review*, 1993.

"Shepherd's Pie" first appeared in *Lit A'la Carte: Favorite Recipes of the Famous Authors* (Bayside Press, 1995).

"Monahsetah" and "Sand Creek, Colorado" were first published in *Greyhounding This America* (Heidelberg Graphics, 1988).

"New Song," "Roman Nose" and "O/Rain-in-the-Face" first appeared in *In the Time of the Present* (Michigan State U Press, 2000).

"I, Tekonwatonti," and "Molly At His Death" first appeared in
Tekonwatonti: Molly Brant (White Pine Press, 1992).

"Stone Throwing" first appeared in *Carving Hawk: New and Selected Poems* (White Pine Press, 2002).

"I Am the Sun" first appeared in *I Am the Sun* (1976).

"The Dugout" first appeared in *The Short and the Long of It* (1990).

"Horses" first appeared in *The Smell of Slaughter* (1982).

"Moccasin" first appeared in *Dancing Back Strong the Nation* (White Pine Press, 1981).

"Little Big Horn" and "Listening to Leslie Marmon Silko" first appeared in *Humours and/or Not So Humorous* (Swift Kick Press, 1988)

"Archaeologist" first appeared in *On Second Thought*, (University of Oklahoma Press, 1995).

"The Murder of Jack Smith" originally appeared in "Confluencia Magazine" and was reprinted in *Backward to Forward* (White Pine Press, 1997).

Several poems included here are reprinted from earlier publications by White Pine Press. I offer a special thanks to the editors of White Pine, Dennis and Elaine Maloney, who have done so much for me for decades.

In addition, many people need to be thanked for their encouragement or subsistence during the actual research and writing of much of the material: Alice Sharp, Reference Librarian of the Colorado State Historical Society in Denver; Dr. Peter Hoch and his late wife; the late Alfred H. Hoch; Lanslott Jones; and the late Willard Motley who told me to write, write and write some more and gave me a bed in the pink house on the hill overlooking Mexico City; Alma Reed who was the author of so many fine archaeological books and especially her biography of Orozco, the Mexican muralist; and editors Bro. Benet Tvedten of the "Blue Cloud Quarterly"; Patricia Andrea; Paula Gunn Allen; Geary Hobson; Elizabeth Cook-Lynn; Sarah Iselin; Sue Shotwell of the Black Kettle Museum in Cheyenne, Oklahoma; Winston Leyland who commissioned "Tinseled Bucks"; Michael Castro; Joseph Bruchac; James Ruppert; Elaine and Dennis Maloney again, with Steve Lewandowski for their faith; and the late Louis Cook who made so much possible with his particular expertise and genius; of course my college professors Werner Beyer and Douglas Angus who taught me how to dot my "i" and cross my "t"; and I must not forget my dear friends Wanda McCaddon and Julian Block; and my niece, Martha and her husband Steve; and for all the joy and natural gifts of life I wish to sincerely and deeply show my appreciation by thanking my lovely Aunt Jennie Sanford of Three Mile Bay, NY. Much of what I do and have accomplished and will continue to create is without a doubt because of her loving care as a small child on her farm. And thanks to Cecilia Martin, my typist, and to Chad Sweeney, my editor, collaborator, and former student. And to the poet Wendy Rose.

BIBLIOGRAPHY

Agonito, Joseph. *Brave Hearts: Indian Women of the Plains.* Guilford Connecticut: Twodot Books, 2017.

Ambrose, Stephen E. *Crazy Horse & Custer.* NY: Meridian, 1986.

Barnitz, Albert & Jeannie. *Life In Custer's Cavalry: Diaries and Letters of 1867-1868.* Lincoln: Bison Books, U Nebraska P, 1977.

Berthrong, Donald. *The Southern Cheyenne.* Norman: U Oklahoma P, 1963.

Brill, Charles J. *Conquest Of The Southern Plains.* Oklahoma City C., 1928.

Connell, Evan S.: *Son Of The Morning Star: Custer & The Little Big Horn.* San Francisco: North Point Press, 1984.

Custer, Elizabeth. *Following the Guidon.* Intro. Jane A. Stewart. Norman: U Oklahoma P, 1966.

Custer, George Armstrong. *My Life On The Plains.* Lincoln: Bison Books, U Nebraska P, 1969.

Epple, Jess C. "Custer's Battle Of The Washita." *Exposition*, NY, 1970.

Gage, Duncan. "Black Kettle: A Noble Savage," *Chronicles of Oklahoma,* Vol XLV # 3, 1967.

Garrard, Lewis. *Wah-To-Yah and the Taos Trail.* Norman: U Oklahoma P, 1962.

Graham, W.A. Colonel. *The Custer Myth.* NY: Bonanza Books, 1953.

Grinnell, George Bird. *The Cheyenne Indians.* Lincoln: U Nebraska P, 1972.

_____. *The Fighting Cheyenne.* Norman: U Oklahoma P, 1966.

Harrison, Peter. Monahsetah: *The Life of a Custer Captive.* Southampton: Chetwynd Press, 2014.

Hazen, W.B., "Some Corrections of 'My Life On The Plains.'" *Chronicles of Oklahoma,* Vol. 3 # 3, 1925.

Hoig, Stan. *The Battle of the Washita.* Lincoln: Bison Books / U Nebraska P, 1979.

_____. *The Sand Creek Massacre*. Norman: U Oklahoma P, 1961.

_____. Tribal Wars of the Southern Plains. Norman, OK: U Oklahoma P, 1993.

Hyde, George E. *The Life of George Bent: Written from His Letters*. Ed. Savoie Lottinville. Norman: U Oklahoma P, 1967.

Jones, Douglas O. *The Treaty of Medicine Lodge*. Norman: U Oklahoma P, 1966.

Kammen, Robert; Lefthand, Frederick; Marshall, Joe. *Soldiers Falling into Camp: The Battle of the Little Big Horn*. Wyoming: Affiliated Writers of America Publishers, 1992.

Keim, De B. Randolph. Sheridan's Troopers on the Border: *A Winter Campaign on the Plains*. Philadelphia: David McKay Books, 1889.

Kidd, J.H. *A Cavalryman with Custer.* NY: Bantam Books, 1991.

Kinsley, D.A. *Favor The Bold*; *Vol 2*. New York: Hold, Rinehart and Winston, 1968.

Lavendar, David. *Bent's Fort*. New York: Doubleday, 1954.

Miller, David Humphreys. *Custer's Fall*. New York: Duell, Sloan & Pearce, 1937.

Monaghan, Jay. Custer: The Life of General George Armstrong Custer. Lincoln: Bison Books, U Nebraska P 1971.

Marquis, Thomas B. *She Watched Custer's Last Battle*. Pamphlet. Mardin, Montana: Hardin Tribune-Herald, 1935.

_____. *Wooden Leg, a Warrior Who Fought Custer*. Lincoln: Bison Books, U Nebraska P, 1971.

Murphy, John. "Reminiscences of the Washita Campaign and of the Darlington Indian Agency," *Chronicles of Oklahoma*, Vol 1, # 3, 1923.

Powell, Peter J. *Sweet Medicine: Continuing Role of the Sacred Arrows, the Sun Dance, and the Sacred Buffalo Hat in Northern Cheyenne History*. Norman: U Oklahoma P, 1969.

Rister, Carle Coke. *Border Command: General Phil Sheridan in the West.* Norman: U Oklahoma P, 1944.

Ryan, J.C. *Custer Fell First.* San Antonio: The Naylor Company, 1966.

Sandoz, Mari. *The Battle of the Little Big Horn.* New York: Modern Literary Editions, 1966.

_____. *Cheyenne Autumn.* New York: Hastings House, 1953.

Shirk, George H. "Campaigning with Sheridan: A Farrier's Diary," *Chronicles of Oklahoma*, Vol XXXVLL, # 1, 1959.

Spotts, David L. *Campaigning with Custer 1868-69*, Ed. E.A. Brininstool. Lincoln: Bison Books, U Nebraska P, 1988.

Stanley, Henry M. *My Early Travels and Adventures in America and Asia.* New York: Charles Scribner's & Sons, 1895.

Taylor, William O. *With Custer on the Little Big Horn; A Newly Discovered First Person Account.* Foreword Greg Martin Van Der Water. New York, Viking Books, 1996.

Van de Water, Frederic F. Glory Hunter: A Life of *General George Custer.* Indianapolis: Bobbs Merrill, 1944.

Vestal, Stanley. Warpath of Council Fires. New York: Random House, 1948.

United States Congress, House of Representatives, "Massacre of Cheyenne Indians." Report on the Conduct of the War. 38 Cong., 2 Sets. Washington, DC G.P.O. 1865.

U.S. Congress, Report of the Commission of Indian Affairs, 1871.

United States Senate, "Sand Creek Massacre." Report of the Committee of War, Sen. Exec., Doc. 26, 39 Cong. 2 Sess. Washington, DC, G.P.O. 1867.

United States Commissioner of Indian Affairs Annual Reports, 1860-91.

Utley, Robert M. *Cavalier in Buckskin: George Armstrong Custer and the Western Military Frontier.* Norman: U Oklahoma P, 1989.

Vestal, Stanley. Warpath: *The True story of the Fighting Sioux Told in a Biography of Chief White Bull.* Lincoln: U Nebraska P, 1984.

Walker, Judson Eliot. *Campaigns Of General Custer*. New York, Promontory Press, 1966.

Welch, James with Paul Stecher. *Killing Custer*. New York: W.W. Norton, 1994.

White Bull, Chief Joseph. *The Warrior Who Killed Custer.* Trans. and Ed. James H. Lincoln: Howard, U Nebraska P 1969.

Wynkoop, Lt. Edward W. "Unfinished History of Colorado." State Historical Society of Colorado.

Maurice Kenny is a major Native American author, historian and editor with over fifty collections of poetry and fiction to his name. Kenny earned special renowned for his poetry readings which inspired audiences across the United States and Europe with a blend of humor, lyric intensity and rhythmic oracular chanting. Kenny's generosity was famous among colleagues and students in hosting dinners and discussions at his house and poetry events in the community while teaching poetry and Native history at SUNY Potsdam, University of Oklahoma, Paul Smith's College, North Country Community College, and the En'owkin Center at the University of Victoria in British Columbia. With Joshua Gosciak, he edited the influential *Contact/II Magazine* for twenty years and was publisher and editor of Strawberry Press which featured works by Native writers. Maurice Kenny was educated at Butler, St. Lawrence University, and New York University where he studied with the eminent poet, Louise Bogan. Twice nominated for the Pulitzer Prize and inducted into the New York Writers Hall of Fame, Maurice Kenny's awards include an American Book Award for *The Mama Poems* (1984), A National Public Radio Award for Broadcasting for a radio production of his poem *"The Dugout,"* the Lifetime Achievement Award from the Native Writers' Circle of the Americas, the Elder Recognition Award from Wordcraft Circle of Native Writers, and a Lila Wallace Reader's Digest Writers' Award for which he toured nationally with Carolyn Forché. He was also awarded an honorary doctorate from St. Lawrence University. After retiring from SUNY Potsdam in 2011, he returned to his beloved Saranac Lake where he passed away in April of 2016 at the age of 86.

Chad Sweeney is the author of seven books of poetry and translation and two edited editions. Sweeney's poems have appeared widely, including in *Best American Poetry*, *The Pushcart Prize Anthology and The Writer's Almanac*. He holds a Ph.D. from Western Michigan University and an  M.F.A. from San Francisco State University. He teaches poetry at California State University San Bernardino and lives in Redlands, CA.

www.ingramcontent.com/pod-product-compliance
Lightning Source LLC
Chambersburg PA
CBHW030831020726
47499CB00006B/2154